CONTENTS

D1512337

Japanese
made easy

Revised Edition

Tazuko Ajiro Monane
Updated, revised and illustrated by Yumi Matsunari

TUTTLE PUBLISHING
Tokyo • Rutland, Vermont • Singapore

Published by Tuttle Publishing, an imprint of Periplus Editions (HK) Ltd., with editorial offices at 364 Innovation Drive, North Clarendon, Vermont 05759 U.S.A., and at 61 Tai Seng Avenue #02-12, Singapore 534167

Library of Congress Cataloging-in-Publication Data
Monane, Tazuko Ajiro.
  Japanese made easy / by Tazuko Ajiro Monane. -- Rev. ed. / updated and revised by Yumi Matsunari.
     p. cm.
  Includes indexes.
  ISBN 978-4-8053-0963-6 (pbk.)
  1. Japanese language--Textbooks for foreign speakers. I. Matsunari, Yumi. II. Title.
  PL539.3.M66 2009
  495.6'83421--dc22
                              2009013945

ISBN-13: 978-4-8053-0963-6

495.683
WITHDRAWN

Distributed by

North America, Latin America & Europe
Tuttle Publishing
364 Innovation Drive
North Clarendon, VT 05759-9436 U.S.A.
Tel: 1 (802) 773-8930; Fax: 1 (802) 773-6993
info@tuttlepublishing.com
www.tuttlepublishing.com

Japan
Tuttle Publishing
Yaekari Building, 3rd Floor
5-4-12 Osaki
Shinagawa-ku
Tokyo 141 0032
Tel: (81) 3 5437-0171; Fax: (81) 3 5437-0755
tuttle-sales@gol.com

Asia Pacific
Berkeley Books Pte. Ltd.
61 Tai Seng Avenue #02-12
Singapore 534167
Tel: (65) 6280-1330; Fax: (65) 6280-6290
inquiries@periplus.com.sg
www.periplus.com

First revised edition
14 13 12 11 10   10 9 8 7 6 5 4 3 2 1

Printed in Singapore

TUTTLE PUBLISHING* is a registered trademark of Tuttle Publishing, a division of Periplus Editions (HK) Ltd.

ACKNOWLEDGMENTS

I should like to express my warm thanks most of all to my students, who have taught me the importance of placing in real-life situations each language pattern they learn. Their interest and motivation to learn when language comes situationally alive has been a major inspiration for me in preparing this book.

I am deeply indebted to Mrs Pamela Miller for her help with the initial editing. The ideas, suggestions, and encouragement of my husband, Dr Joseph Monane, have been a constant source of support. Finally, I should like to express my appreciation to the Charles E. Tuttle Company, whose receptivity to the format of this book has been a warm and gratifying experience.

—TAZUKO AJIRO MONANE

I would like to thank all the editors and designers at Tuttle Publishing, especially Eric Oey, Bob Graham, Nancy Goh, and Angie Ang, for inviting me to participate in this project and assisting me in my efforts. The core of the late Dr. Tazuko Monane's work is timeless, and is as valuable for today's students as when it was first written. It has been an honor for me to revise the work to reflect current language usage, and I have done my best to do so in a manner that is sensitive to the integrity of the original material. I would also like to thank my sons, James and Luke, for their love and support.

—YUMI MATSUNARI

STUDY SUGGESTIONS

Japanese Made Easy is a basic, do-it-yourself guide to the Japanese language and is designed for people living in or going to Japan who have never studied Japanese before. Obviously, living or traveling in Japan is itself not the secret of learning Japanese—many foreigners live in Japan for a long time and except for a few words learn very little about its language. The important thing will be your motivation to learn. Whether you go to Japan as a tourist, student, or businessperson, whether you use this book before or after your arrival in Japan, what could provide better motivation than knowing that a familiarity with the Japanese language (and with the culture it reflects) will help make your stay in Japan much richer and much more interesting.

If you have the good fortune to know a Japanese person, he or she will surely make your learning even easier—especially when you study pronunciation. But don't be discouraged if you have no "live model" to learn from. By following the simple suggestions given here, you will be able to come out with good, understandable Japanese on your own. Here are some ideas, then, for how you can get the most out of this book.

Chapters and lessons

This book contains ten chapters. Each chapter contains an introduction, dialogue, and several lessons. The introduction provides a brief overview of the sentence patterns that appear in the chapter. The dialogue is a short conversation in standard modern Japanese. It presents examples of sentence pattern usage in the context of everyday Japanese conversations. The dialogue is first presented in native Japanese script, followed by romanized Japanese (*romaji*) and English. It should be read through quickly at first, and then returned to for review after the chapter lessons have been completed. If possible, practice the dialogues with a friend or native speaker, memorizing them as best you can.

Each chapter contains several lessons, each of which focuses on a situation that you are likely to encounter in Japan. Because the vocabulary, sentence patterns, explanations, and practice sections all work together to present the basics of the Japanese language in the context of a single situation, each lesson should be studied as a complete unit. This introduction of new language patterns within common situations is a basic principle that helps all learners, and it should help you to develop a real feel for the material you study.

As your confidence grows through mastering the basic patterns provided herein, you will discover that the patterns are applicable in many more situations than those covered in the book. Though you should, in the beginning, confine yourself to the material in each lesson, try later on to make up new situations on your own to see if you can handle them in Japanese.

Japanese script versus romaji

Japanese script (a combination of *hiragana, katakana,* and basic *kanji*) has been added throughout the new edition of the book. Although reading and writing are not taught herein, it is hoped that the inclusion of Japanese script will be useful to those that have just started learning or are already somewhat familiar with the Japanese writing system. If you already know hiragana and katakana (collectively known as *kana*), comparing the Japanese and romaji scripts will help you to learn some new kanji at the same time that you are mastering the sentence patterns. If you haven't yet learned kana, don't let that slow you down. Stick to the romaji and focus on mastering the sentence patterns for now. Later, you can easily learn the kana and then use the Japanese scripts for review.

Vocabulary lists

The words used in each dialogue and lesson, plus other important words that will be good to know, are introduced in the vocabulary lists in each chapter. Depending on the amount of time you can spend, choose words to remember that you feel will be of most use to you. Go over the vocabulary lists often and try to make up sentences of your own. Just learning the words themselves will not be of great help to you. Remember that words are almost always used in sentences!

The supplementary vocabulary (Appendix 1) will give you some additional words that you can use to help strengthen your speaking and comprehension skills.

Culture and vocabulary notes

These notes will explain some specific vocabulary items and help you to see how the Japanese language operates in context. They will often highlight how certain features of the language relate to Japanese culture. Generally, only basic, easily understood information is given here.

Sentence patterns

Devote most of your study to sentence patterns. The ones I have selected for you are the core of the Japanese language. They are the building-blocks of a solid foundation onto which you can add, for each sentence pattern can be used in many different ways.

So approach each sentence pattern with patience. Practice it thoroughly before going on in the book. Use it as often as you can as a base for longer utterances of several sentences so that you avoid the choppy style that comes from using a sentence in isolation.

Sentence patterns throughout are numbered for your convenience. You will find the related forms of a basic sentence pattern marked A, B, or C. For example, 30A, 30B, and 30C are not three sentence patterns but simply variations of Sentence Pattern 30. Studying these as group will make your learning a good deal easier.

Practice sections

Practice sections form the concluding part of each lesson. Answers to all questions are provided near the back of the book.

In addition, whenever you learn a new sentence pattern, try to practice it from several angles. For example:

1. Try carrying on dialogues with yourself. Play both person's roles in these conversations. Even better, try to find a partner who will do this with you.
2. See whether you can ask questions in Japanese. Tape yourself saying these questions on a recorder and then try to answer them in Japanese.
3. Try describing the things around you.
4. See whether you can express what you're going to do, what you've done, what you usually do, and so on.

If you're resourceful when doing the above, it can be fun as well as a good way to learn.

Review

Before you go on to a new chapter be sure to go over what you've learned so that you know it thoroughly. Look at the dialogues and vocabulary lists often. Repeat sentences to yourself while driving your car or riding the bus or subway. If you're studying in Japan, find social situations in which you can use your Japanese. Be outgoing. Ask directions, even when you know the right way to go.

Useful expressions

A group of useful, everyday expressions (greetings and the like) is given in Chapter 10. These expressions have been placed here because they are idiomatic, specialized phrases and need to be memorized. But there is no reason for you to wait until you reach Chapter 10 before you begin to learn to use them. You might study Lesson 1 of Chapter 10 along with Chapters 1 and 2, Lesson 2 of Chapter 10 along with Chapters 3 and 4, and so on. Studying Chapter 10 in this way will reduce the amount of material to memorize at one time, and it will give you many helpful expressions to use (and the ability to recognize when others use them) early in your learning.

Few foreigners in Japan take the trouble to become fluent in Japanese. Don't be surprised if you find many Japanese people, pleased with your efforts, complimenting you even when you've achieved what you know to be a bare minimum of competence. Don't be spoiled by this and be content to stop where you are in your learning. Accept the morale-boost this kind of compliment can bring, but let your reach always exceed your present grasp so that you can continue to advance in your conversational skills.

Going to Japanese movies, watching Japanese TV programs, eavesdropping on conversations in Japanese (difficult to do, but when you can do it successfully you've really learned!), starting conversations with Japanese people (don't hesitate to do this; you'll find that Japanese will often initiate conversations in English with you)—all of these will be helpful to you. And don't be afraid of making mistakes. Japanese people will never ridicule you or make you feel embarrassed.

After completing this book you will find yourself able to shop, order drinks and meals, buy tickets, travel, and generally make yourself understood anywhere in Japan. You will be able to explore Japan on your own instead of being totally dependent on tours and planned excursions, and this will bring you many gratifying experiences you might otherwise miss. What's more, by completing this book you will have demonstrated that you have the ability to be a serious student of Japanese, and you will be in a good position to continue your study should you wish.

Many Westerners think Oriental languages are very difficult to learn. I hope that through this simple, easy-to-use guide to the Japanese language that I may reach some readers who have had that feeling and help them realize that it is not so.

Good luck! Your diligence will help you understand not only the language but also the people and culture of Japan. I think you'll find they're worth the effort.

—Tazuko Ajiro Monane

PRONUNCIATION GUIDE

Pronunciation of Japanese is relatively easy. Once you acquire basic knowledge about Japanese sounds and master them with the help of a native speaker or with the help of recorded materials, you will not have much difficulty. There are five vowels in Japanese. In this book these vowels are written; **a**, **i**, **u**, **e**, and **o**, or あ, い, う, え and お in hiragana.

a	あ	like the *a* in *ha ha!*
i	い	like the *i* in *Bali*
u	う	like the *u* in *June*, but shorter in length
e	え	like the *e* in *pet*
o	お	like the *o* in *colt*

Long and short vowels

Long vowels are written in this book as ā, ii, ū, ē, and ō. Don't confuse these with what are called long vowels in English. In Japanese, a long vowel is sustained twice as long as a short one, but the sound of the vowel remains the same. Therefore, it is often the length of the vowel that distinguishes one word from another. Note the important difference in meaning made by the short and long vowel in the following pairs.

ob<u>a</u>san	おばさん	aunt	**ob<u>ā</u>san**	おばあさん	grandmother
oj<u>i</u>san	おじさん	uncle	**oj<u>ii</u>san**	おじいさん	grandfather
ku<u>k</u>i	くき	stem	**k<u>ū</u>ki**	くうき	air
<u>e</u>	え	picture	**<u>ē</u>**	ええ	yes
<u>o</u>ku	おく	to put	**<u>ō</u>ku**	おおく	plenty

Syllables

Japanese think of their words as being composed of syllables, each syllable taking one beat. A Japanese syllable may be any one of the following:

1. One short vowel only: **a**, **i**, **u**, **e**, **o**.
2. The first or second half of any long vowel (ā, ii, ū, ē, and ō). Therefore, one long vowel equals two syllables.
3. A consonant + a vowel:

ka	か	ki	き	ku	く	ke	け	ko	こ
sa	さ	shi	し	su	す	se	せ	so	そ
ta	た	chi	ち	tsu	つ	te	て	to	と
na	な	ni	に	nu	ぬ	ne	ね	no	の
ha	は	hi	ひ	fu	ふ	he	へ	ho	ほ
ma	ま	mi	み	mu	む	me	め	mo	も
ya	や	–	–	yu	ゆ	–	–	yo	よ
ra	ら	ri	り	ru	る	re	れ	ro	ろ
ga	が	gi	ぎ	gu	ぐ	ge	げ	go	ご
za	ざ	ji	じ	zu	ず	ze	ぜ	zo	ぞ
da	だ	–	–	–	–	de	で	do	ど
ba	ば	bi	び	bu	ぶ	be	べ	bo	ぼ
pa	ぱ	pi	ぴ	pu	ぷ	pe	ぺ	po	ぽ
ja	じゃ	–	–	ju	じゅ	–	–	jo	じょ
wa	わ	–	–	–	–	–	–	–	–

4. The consonant **n** (ん) (when not attached to a vowel). This syllable only appears:

    (a) at the end of a word: **ho̲n** (book)

    (b) in the middle of a word:

        (i) when followed by a consonant: **ko̲nnichi wa** (hello)

        (ii) when followed by a vowel or **y**:

ki̲n-en きんえん no smoking **u̲n-yu** うんゆ transportation

Failure to pronounce the sounds exactly as marked by the hyphen may change the meaning of the word.

ki̲n-en きんえん no smoking **ki-ne̲n** きねん commemoration
shi̲n-in しんいん new member(s) **shi-ni̲n** しにん dead persons

In some older books, the consonant **n** is written **m** in romaji before the sounds **b**, **m**, and **p**. However, we shall continue to write it as **n** in this book.

sa̲nbyaku さんびゃく three hundred
sa̲nman さんまん thirty thousand
sa̲npo さんぽ walk

5. A combination of sounds: a consonant + the consonant **y** (or **h**) + a vowel:

kya	きゃ	kyu	きゅ	kyo	きょ
sha	しゃ	shu	しゅ	sho	しょ
cha	ちゃ	chu	ちゅ	cho	ちょ
nya	にゃ	nyu	にゅ	nyo	にょ
hya	ひゃ	hyu	ひゅ	hyo	ひょ
mya	みゃ	myu	みゅ	myo	みょ
rya	りゃ	ryu	りゅ	ryo	りょ
gya	ぎゃ	gyu	ぎゅ	gyo	ぎょ
bya	びゃ	byu	びゅ	byo	びょ
pya	ぴゃ	pyu	ぴゅ	pyo	ぴょ

6. The first consonant (only the first) of certain double consonants: **kk, ss, ssh, tt, tch, tts, pp**. Failure to give a full beat to this syllable may change the meaning of the word.

shitte	しって	knowing	shite	して	doing
kitte	きって	a stamp	kite	きて	coming
issho	いっしょ	together	isho	いしょ	last will
hikkaku	ひっかく	to scratch	hikaku	ひかく	comparison
matchi	マッチ	a match	machi	まち	town
itta	いった	went	ita	いた	board, plank

Pronunciation of consonants

1. The Japanese **r** seems to give the most trouble to speakers of other languages. If you pronounce **ra, ri, ru, re**, and **ro** with exactly the same **r** as in English, you will not produce the correct Japanese sound. The Japanese **r** resembles a combination of the English **r** and **l**. So, relax your tongue and first practice saying **la, li, lu, le** and **lo**. Next, close the lips more, hold them fairly steady, and pronounce the same sounds without rolling your tongue. You will be able to produce the correct Japanese **ra, ri, ru, re** and **ro** that way.

2. The Japanese **f** as in **Fuji-san**, "Mt Fuji," is very different from the English **f** in which you touch the lower lip with the upper teeth to get the sound. In Japanese, this is not done. The Japanese **f** is pronounced more like the English **h**.

3. The Japanese final **n** in such words as **hon**, "book," and **Nihon** or **Nippon**, "Japan," is a little different from the English final **n** in which the tongue touches the palate just behind the upper teeth, as in "one" and "ten." The Japanese final **n** is nasalized and more relaxed; the tongue does not touch the upper palate.

4. All other consonants should be pronounced as they are in English.

Pronunciation of syllables

You must learn to pronounce each syllable clearly and with the same amount of stress. Each syllable must be equal in length. Note the number of syllables in the examples below. Remember, each syllable gets one beat, so a long vowel gets counted as two syllables. Give one beat to the consonant **n** and to the first consonant of the double consonant.

Ohayō.	おはよう。	o-ha-yo-o *(4)*	Good morning.
Ohayō	おはよう	o-ha-yo-o-	Good morning.
gozaimasu.	ございます。	go-za-i-ma-su *(9)*	
Konnichi wa.	こんにちは。	ko-n-ni-chi-wa *(5)*	Hello.
Konban wa.	こんばんは。	ko-n-ba-n-wa *(5)*	Good evening.
hikkaku	ひっかく	hi-k-ka-ku *(4)*	to scratch

Don't put a heavy stress on any syllable. Particularly avoid the "potato" accent (a heavy stress on the second syllable of a three-syllable word) and the "macaroni" accent (a heavy stress on the third syllable of a four-syllable word). Practice the following proper names.

Matsui	まつい	Hashimoto	はしもと
Nakao	なかお	Matsumoto	まつもと
Tanaka	たなか	Takahashi	たかはし
Yamada	やまだ	Yamanaka	やまなか

Remember: keep each syllable clear, equal in length, and even in stress.

Phrasing

In English, a preposition such as "in," "for," "of," or "at" is usually pronounced as a single unit: "in the ocean," "during my vacation," "for the company," "at seven o'clock." In Japanese, a particle (which often follows a noun) is pronounced as a part of the noun or noun phrase that precedes it. In the following sentence, a slash indicates the correct phrasing.

Kōhii o / kudasai.	コーヒーを／ ください。	Please give me a cup of coffee.
Sukiyaki ga /tabetai desu.	すきやきが／ たべたいです。	I want to eat *sukiyaki*.
Nara e / ikitai desu.	ならへ／いきたいです。	I want to go Nara.

If you get used to this phrasing, you can perceive each of the three sentence above as comprising two units rather than three—which makes your learning much easier. (Think how easy it is to learn telephone numbers when you think of them not as seven separate digits but as two units—three digits plus four digits, as in 555-3561.)

This phrasing rule is one of the most important in Japanese. In the numbered sentence-pattern models you will be studying, the phrasing is clearly marked with a slash. You need not always pause while speaking, but if you do, make sure that the pause comes where it is marked in the sentence patterns in this book. Your Japanese will sound much more natural to Japanese ears.

Chapter 1
(Lessons 1 – 4)

Sentence Patterns Covered in Chapter 1		
Sentence Pattern 1	NOUN + o / kudasai.	〜を ください。
Sentence Pattern 1A	NOUN + to + NOUN + o / kudasai.	〜と 〜を ください。
	NOUN + to + NOUN + to + NOUN + o / kudasai.	〜と 〜と 〜を ください。
Sentence Pattern 1B	Kore o / kudasai.	これを ください。
	Sore o / kudasai.	それを ください。
	Are o / kudasai.	あれを ください。
	Kono + NOUN + o / kudasai.	この〜を ください。
	Sono + NOUN + o / kudasai.	その〜を ください。
	Ano + NOUN + o / kudasai.	あの〜を ください。

Many words borrowed from other languages (mostly English) are used frequently in Japanese. Several of these will be introduced in this chapter to give you an immediate working vocabulary that you can easily retain and use with confidence in many situations. These borrowed words will also give you practice in Japanese pronunciation.

It is absolutely essential to practice these Japanese borrowed words with the correct Japanese pronunciation. As Jack Seward* points out, the average citizen of Japan, upon hearing a Westerner (who is usually presumed to be an American) having difficulty speaking Japanese, often attempts to give that foreigner a helping hand by injecting as many borrowed words as he can into his own speech. The result is generally disastrous.

This kindness would be beneficial if the borrowed words were used and pro-

---

* Jack Seward, *Japanese in Action* (New York: Walker/ Weatherhill 1969), p. 98.

nounced in Japanese as they are used and pronounced in the language from which they were borrowed. Unfortunately, they seldom are, and the Westerner is more confused than ever. Let's look at some situations in which these borrowed words are frequently used.

Dialogue

Waitress	：	何にしましょうか？
田中	：	コーヒーをください。
山田	：	アップルジュースとパンをください。
田中	：	私もパンをください。

山田	：	それは何ですか？
Waitress	：	これはブルベリチーズケーキです。
山田	：	それをください。
田中	：	あの赤いケーキは何ですか？
Waitress	：	あれはラズベリーチーズケーキです。
田中	：	じゃあ、あのケーキをください。

Waitress	:	**Nani ni shimashō ka?**	What shall I bring you?
Tanaka	:	**Kōhii o kudasai.**	Please bring me coffee.
Yamada	:	**Appuru jūsu to pan o kudasai.**	Please bring me apple juice and bread.
Tanaka	:	**Watashi mo pan o kudasai.**	Please bring bread to me too.

Yamada	:	Sore wa nan desuka?	What is that (close to you)?
Waitress	:	Kore wa buruberii chiizukēki desu.	This (close to me) is blueberry cheesecake.
Yamada	:	Sore o kudasai.	Please give me that (close to you).
Tanaka	:	Ano akai kēki wa nan desuka?	What is that red cake (over there)?
Waitress	:	Are wa razuberii chiizukēki desu.	That (over there) is raspberry cheesecake.
Tanaka	:	Jā, ano kēki o kudasai.	Well, then, please bring me that cake (over there).

Dialogue vocabulary

akai	赤い	red
ano/are	あの／あれ	that (over there)
appuru jūsu	アップルジュース	apple juice
buruberi chiizukēki	ブルベリチーズ ケーキ	blueberry cheesecake
desu	です	is/are
jā	じゃあ	Well, then …
kēki	ケーキ	cake
kōhii	コーヒー	coffee
kono/kore	この／これ	this (by me)
mo	も	too
nani/nan	何	What?
pan (from Portuguese pāo)	パン	bread
~ o kudasai.	〜 を ください。	Please give/bring me ~.
razuberii chiizukēki	ラズベリーチーズ ケーキ	raspberry cheesecake
shimashō ka?	しましょうか	will you have/will you do?
sono/sore	その／それ	that (by you)
watashi	私	I

Culture and vocabulary notes

Jā is often used at the beginning of sentence in the same way that "well" or "well then" is used in English. **Watakushi** is a more formal word for "I" or "me" than **watashi**. The particle **mo** adds the meaning *too* or *also*. Thus the expression **watashi mo** can be translated as "Me too."

Ordering at a Coffee Shop

In this lesson, you will learn a sentence pattern that will permit you to order various items at a restaurant or shop. You will also learn the Japanese words for many basic food items.

Vocabulary

aisu kōhii	アイスコーヒー	iced coffee
aisukuriimu	アイスクリーム	ice cream
aisukuriimu sōda	アイスクリーム ソーダ	ice cream soda
aisu tii	アイスティー	iced tea
appuru pai	アップルパイ	apple pie
batā	バター	butter
chokorēto sheiku	チョコレート シェイク	chocolate shake
hamu sandoitchi (hamu sando)*	ハムサンドイッチ (ハムサンド)	ham sandwich
jūsu	ジュース	juice
kōcha	紅茶	black tea
kōra	コーラ	cola
kokoa	ココア	cocoa
mikkusu sandoitchi (mikkusu sando)	ミックスサンドイッチ (ミックスサンド)	combination sandwich (usually ham, cheese, egg and tomato)
miruku	ミルク	milk
mizu	水	water (cold)
ocha	お茶	tea (any kind)
omuraisu	オムライス	rice omelet
orenji jūsu	オレンジ ジュース	orange juice
pai	パイ	pie
remonēdo	レモネード	lemonade
sandoitchi (sando)	サンドイッチ	sandwich
sōda	ソーダ	soda
tomato jūsu	トマト ジュース	tomato juice

* A Japanese word in parentheses after the main entry is an alternate form or a word of the same meaning but of less frequent occurrence.

Culture and vocabulary notes

Coffee shops or tea rooms, called **kissaten** (喫茶店), are numerous in Japan and are very popular places to meet friends and relax. You can order all kinds of soft drinks, desserts, and even light-lunch items such as sandwiches there. Many of these items are foreign loanwords and so are written in katakana.

In any situation that involves buying or shopping, **kudasai** can mean "Please bring (me)," "Please sell (me)," or "Please give (me)." The *o* in **Kōhii *o* kudasai** is called a particle. It has no meaning in itself but indicates that the preceding word is the direct object in the sentence. Other particles will be introduced later.

There are no articles like "a" or "the" in Japanese. Although in English you tend to say, "Please give me *some* ice cream," Japanese usually just say, "Please give me ice cream."

Grammar

The first sentence pattern below shows you the simplest way to ask for something in Japanese. It consists of the item (a noun) you want, a particle, and a word meaning "please." Look carefully at the sentence pattern that follows.

Sentence Pattern 1	
NOUN + o / kudasai. 〜を ください。	Please give me + NOUN.

Examples

Sōda o kudasai. ソーダをください。	Please give me soda.
Jūsu o kudasai. ジュースをください。	Please give me juice.
Kēki o kudasai. ケーキをください。	Please give me cake.
Aisukuriimu o kudasai. アイスクリームをください。	Please give me ice cream.
Kokoa o kudasai. ココアをください。	Please give me cocoa.
Chokorēto sheiku o kudasai. チョコレートシェイクをください。	Please give me (a) chocolate shake.

Practice

1. Practice saying these sentences aloud. What the waitress says is included for your recognition, since you will hear it often in coffee shops and other places serving the public.

Waitress:

Nani ni shimashō ka?	What shall I bring you?
何にしましょうか？	
[or]	[or]
Nani ni nasaimasu ka?	What are you going to have?
何になさいますか？	

Customer:

Kōhii o kudasai.	Please give me (some) coffee.
コーヒーをください。	
Appuru pai o kudasai.	Please give me (a piece of) apple pie.
アップルパイをください。	
Aisukuriimu o kudasai.	Please give me (some) ice cream.
アイスクリームをください。	
Kōra o kudasai.	Please give me (a) cola.
コーラをください。	
Miruku o kudasai.	Please give me (some) milk.
ミルクをください。	
Orenji jūsu o kudasai.	Please give me (some) orange juice.
オレンジジュースをください。	

2. See if you can order the following items. Turn to page 236 to see the answers.

   a) coffee   b) sandwich   c) lemonade   d) ice cream soda   e) tea

Ordering at a Bar

In this section you will use the sentence pattern from Lesson 1 to order various types of drinks at a bar.

Vocabulary

biiru	ビール	beer
burandē	ブランデー	brandy
jin fuizu	ジンフィズ	gin fizz
kakuteru	カクテル	cocktail
ramu	ラム	rum
Sukotchi uisukii	スコッチウイスキー	Scotch whiskey
uisukii	ウイスキー	whiskey
uisukii sōda	ウイスキーソーダ	whiskey and soda
uokka	ウオッカ	vodka

Useful Expressions

mizuwari de	水割りで	with water and ice
sutorēto de	ストレートで	straight

Culture and Vocabulary Notes

Bars (バー), often called **nomiya** (飲み屋), are popular places for Japanese people to meet for social gatherings with friends or with fellow employees after work. **Izakaya** (居酒屋) are a popular type of pub that also serves simple food.

Mizuwari is a native Japanese word. The *de* in **mizuwari** *de* and **sutorēto de** is a particle that indicates the style of the drink, or how it is to be made. These phrases can be inserted into Sentence Pattern 1.

Grammar

Sukotchi uisukii o kudasai.　　　　Please give me a Scotch.
スコッチウイスキーをください。

Sukotchi uisukii o mizuwari de kudasai. スコッチウイスキーを水割りで ください。	Please give me a Scotch with water and ice.

A sentence like the one immediately above has two particles. One, the particle *o*, shows what you wish to receive. The other, the particle *de,* here shows "how" you want to receive it. The particle *de* has other uses which will be covered later in this book.

Practice

1. Practice using Sentence Pattern 1. Note that the bartender's question below is the same as the waitress' on page 20, but the translation is different. What is important to learn is the intention of the speaker, and this is something that is often not clearly shown in a literal translation. Note these differences as you work through this book.

Bartender:

Nani ni shimashō ka? 何にしましょうか？	What will you have?

Customer:

Uisukii sōda o kudasai. ウイスキーソーダをください。	Please give me a whiskey and soda.
Biiru o kudasai. ビールをください。	Please give me a beer.
Sukotchi uisukii o mizuwari de kudasai. スコッチウイスキーを水割り でください。	Please give me a Scotch with water and ice.
Uisukii o sutorēto de kudasai. ウイスキーをストレートで ください。	Please give me a straight Scotch.

2. See if you can order the following bar items. Turn to page 236 to see the answers.

   a) beer   b) Scotch with water and ice   c) brandy   d) Scotch straight

Ordering at a Restaurant

In this lesson you will learn how to order food at a restaurant. You will also learn how to order two or more items at the same time.

Vocabulary

yōshoku	洋食	Western-style food

Main Dishes

bifuteki (biifusutēki)	ビフテキ (ビーフステーキ)	beefsteak
biifu karē	ビーフカレー	beef curry
biifu shichū	ビーフシチュー	beef stew
chikin karē	チキンカレー	chicken curry
hanbāgā	ハンバーガー	hamburger
karē raisu	カレーライス	curry rice
korokke	コロッケ	croquette
rōsuto biifu	ローストビーフ	roast beef
rōsuto pōku	ローストポーク	roast pork
sarada	サラダ	salad
shiifūdo karē	シーフードカレー	seafood curry
sūpu	スープ	soup
tonkatsu	トンカツ	pork cutlet

Breakfast Items

bēkon	ベーコン	bacon
hamu	ハム	ham
omuretsu	オムレツ	omelet
sōsēji	ソーセージ	sausage

Culture and vocabulary notes

Notice that all of the dishes listed above are foreign loanwords and are written in katakana. As you'll discover in the next chapter, there are many Japanese dishes, such as sushi (寿司), teppanyaki (鉄板焼き), and tenpura (天ぷら), that are written in kanji and/or hiragana.

It is polite to say **itadakimasu** (頂きます) just before beginning a meal to express your appreciation for the food and **gochisōsama deshita** (御馳走さまでした) when you are done to thank your host for the meal.

Grammar

To order two or more items, you need to know the Japanese expression that is equivalent to the English word "and." Though in English you say, "Give me A, B, C, and D," in Japanese you say, 'Give me A and B and C and D."

"And" in Japanese is expressed by the particle *to*. The function of *to* in Japanese is to connect words or phrases, but not clauses or sentences.

Sentence Pattern 1A	
NOUN + **to** + NOUN + **o** / **kudasai.** NOUN + と + NOUN + をください。	Please give me + NOUN + and + NOUN.
NOUN + **to** + NOUN + **to** + NOUN + **o** / **kudasai.** NOUN + と + NOUN + と + NOUN + をください	Please give me + NOUN + NOUN + and + NOUN.

Examples

Hanbāgā to kōhii o kudasai.
ハンバーガーとコーヒーをください。

Please give me a hamburger and coffee.

Omuretsu to jūsu to kōhii o kudasai.
オムレツとジュースとコーヒーをください。

Please give me an omelet, juice, and coffee.

Practice

1. Practice saying the following sentences aloud.

Waitress:
Nani ni shimashō ka?
何にしましょうか？

What shall I bring you?

Customer:
Biifu karē to sarada o kudasai.
ビーフカレーとサラダをください。

Please bring me beef curry and salad.

Hanbāgā to biiru o kudasai.
ハンバーガーとビールをください。

Please bring me a hamburger and a beer.

Sarada to miruku o kudasai.
サラダとミルクをください。

Please bring me a salad and some milk.

2. See if you can order two items at the same time in a coffee shop or a bar. Turn to page 236 to see the answers.

    a) coffee and cake
    b) milk and a ham sandwich
    c) coffee and salad
    d) lemonade and a piece of apple pie
    e) gin fizz and beer

Shopping at a Department Store

Here you will learn how to request various items at a department store. You will also learn the noun and adjectival forms of the Japanese expressions for this (by me), that (by you) and that (over there).

Vocabulary

dejitaru kamera	デジタルカメラ	digital camera
diibiidii pureiyā	DVD プレーヤー	DVD player
doresu	ドレス	dress
hankachi	ハンカチ	handkerchief
kādegan	カーディガン	cardigan
kamera	カメラ	camera
konpyūta	コンピュータ	computer
kōto	コート	coat
nekutai	ネクタイ	necktie
rajio	ラジオ	radio
reinkōto (renkoto)	レインコート（レンコート）	raincoat
sētā	セーター	sweater
shatsu	シャツ	undershirt
shiidii	CD	CD
shiidii pureiyā	CD プレーヤー	CD player
sukāfu	スカーフ	scarf
sukāto	スカート	skirt
surakkusu	スラックス	slacks
sutereo	ステレオ	stereo set
sūtsu	スーツ	suit
tabako	タバコ	pack of cigarettes
terebi	テレビ	television set
waishatsu	ワイシャツ	dress shirt

Culture and vocabulary notes

The word **shatsu** usually refers only to an undershirt. If you want to refer to a long-sleeved dress shirt of the sort worn with a suit, use the word **waishatsu**. Depending on the type of shirt, there are also such words as **supōtsu shatsu**, "sports shirt," **aroha shatsu**, "aloha shirt," and so on.

If you use the word **pantsu** to indicate a pair of slacks, you may produce giggles from a Japanese person. **Pantsu** generally means "underwear." The Japanese word for men's "pants" is **zubon**.

Grammar

When shopping in Japan, you may not always know the correct word for the item you wish to buy. In such cases, of course, you can just point to the item and use words for "this" or "that." Sometimes, though, you will know the Japanese word for the item but will wish to specify which among several is the particular one you want.

In English, the sentences "Please give me this" and "Please give me this camera" both use the same word, "this," to specify the item you want. In Japanese, however, the noun and adjective forms of "this" (and "that") are different. Look at the following sentence pattern.

Sentence Pattern 1B	
Kore o / kudasai. これをください。	Please give this (near me) to me.
Sore o / kudasai. それをください。	Please give that (near you) to me.
Are o / kudasai. あれをください。	Please give that (over there) to me.
Kono + NOUN + **o / kudasai** この + NOUN + をください。	Please give me this (near me) + NOUN.
Sono + NOUN + **o / kudasai.** その + NOUN + をください。	Please give me that (near you) + NOUN.
Ano + NOUN + **o / kudasai.** あの + NOUN + をください。	Please give me that (over there) + NOUN.

Examples

Kore o kudasai. これをください。	Please give this (these) to me.
Kono kamera o kudasai. このカメラをください。	Please give me this (these) camera(s) (close to me).
Sono kamera o kudasai. そのカメラをください。	Please give me that (the, those) camera(s) (close to you).
Ano kamera o kudasai. あのカメラをください。	Please give me that (those) camera(s) (some distance from you and me).

Kore, **sore**, and **are** take the place of the noun, just as an English pronoun does. But they are unlike English pronouns in that they have the same form whether the meaning you intend is singular or plural.

Kono, **sono**, and **ano** cannot be used without a following noun. Note, too, that Japanese nouns are unlike most English nouns in that they normally take the same form whether singular or plural.

Use **kore** and **kono** to indicate an object closer to you, the speaker. Use **sore** and **sono** to indicate an object closer to your listener. Use **are** and **ano** to indicate an object that is some distance from both you and your listener.

Practice

1. Practice saying the following sentences aloud.

Clerk:

Nani o sashiagemashō ka? 何をさしあげましょうか？ [or]	What shall I bring you? (polite)
Nani ni shimashō ka? 何にしましょうか？	What can I do for you?

Customer:

Sono reinkōto o kudasai. そのレインコートをください。	Please sell me the raincoat (which is close to you).
Kono sukāfu o kudasai. このスカーフをください。	Please sell me this scarf.
Ano sētā o kudasai. あのセーターをください。	Please sell me that sweater (over there).

Kore o kudasai.　　　　　　　　　Please sell me this.
これをください。

Sore o kudasai.　　　　　　　　　Please sell me that (which is close to
それをください。　　　　　　　　　　you).

2. See if you can shop in a department store by specifying which among several items is the one you want. Turn to page 236 to see the answers.

   a) this necktie

   b) that scarf (over there)

   c) this roll of film

   d) the camera that is close to the clerk

   e) that sweater (over there)

Chapter 2
(Lessons 5 – 10)

Sentence Patterns Covered in Chapter 2		
Sentence Pattern 2	NOUN + ga / + VERB-INFINITIVE + -tai desu.	NOUN + が + VERB-INFINITIVE ＋ たい です。
Sentence Pattern 2A	NOUN + ga / + VERB-INFINITIVE + -tai desu ka?	NOUN + が + VERB-INFINITIVE + たい ですか？
Sentence Pattern 2B	Nani ga / + VERB-INFINITIVE + -tai desu ka? Dore ga / + VERB-INFINITIVE + -tai desu ka?	何が + VERB-INFINITIVE + たいですか？ どれが + VERB-INFINITIVE + たい ですか？
Sentence Pattern 2C	Nani to nani ga / + VERB-INFINITIVE + -tai desu ka? Dore to dore ga / + VERB-INFINITIVE + -tai desu ka?	何と何が + VERB-INFINITIVE + たい ですか？ どれとどれが + VERB-INFINITIVE + たいですか？
Sentence Pattern 3	place + e / ikitai desu.	PLACE + へ行きたい です。
Sentence Pattern 3A	place + e / ikitai desu ka?	PLACE + へ行きたい ですか？
Sentence Pattern 3B	Doko e / ikitai desu ka?	どこへ行きたい ですか？

Sentence Pattern 3C	Doko to doko e / ikitai desu ka?	どことどこへ行きたいですか？
Sentence Pattern 4	Hai (Ē), / + VERB-IN-FINITIVE + -tai desu	はい（えぇ）、+ VERB-INFINITIVE + たいです。
Sentence Pattern 5	Iie, / + verb-infinitive + -taku arimasen.	いいえ、+ VERB-INFINITIVE + たくありません。

In Chapter 1 you were introduced to Japanese words borrowed from other languages. In this chapter you will learn some native Japanese words and the verbs "to eat," "to drink," "to see," "to buy," and "to go." The sentence patterns here will teach you how to express your most basic needs as a traveler in Japan and, just as important, how to find out what your Japanese friends want to do. The chapter will end at a sushi shop, where you will have the chance to select and sample some of the many kinds of fish used in this exquisite cuisine.

Dialogue
真理：何が食べたいですか？
健司：カレーライスが食べたいです。
真理：私はオムライスが食べたいです。
健司：後でどこへ行きたいですか？
真理：そうですね。テレビが見たいですか？

健司：いいえ、見たくありません。
真理：映画が見たいですか？
健司：はい、見たいです。どれが見たいですか？
真理：ロマンチックな映画が見たいです。
健司：私はアニメの映画が見たいです。
真理：見たくありません！

Mari :	Nani ga tabetai desu ka?	What do you want to eat?
Kenji :	Karē raisu ga tabetai desu.	I want to eat a curry and rice dish.
Mari :	Watashi wa omuraisu ga tabetai desu.	I want to eat an omelet and rice dish.
Kenji :	Ato de doko e ikitai desu ka?	Where do you want to go after?
Mari :	Sō desu nē. Terebi ga mitai desu ka?	Hmm. Do you want to watch television?
Kenji :	Iie, mitaku arimasen.	No, I don't want to watch (it).
Mari :	Eiga ga mitai desu ka?	Do you want to see a movie?
Kenji :	Hai, mitai desu. Dore ga mitai desu ka?	Yes, I'd like to see one. Which do you want to see?
Mari :	Romanchikku na eiga ga mitai desu.	I'd like to see a romantic film.
Kenji :	Watashi wa anime no eiga ga mitai desu.	I'd like to see an anime movie.
Mari :	Mitaku arimasen!	I don't want to see (that)!

Dialogue vocabulary

ato	あと	after; later
doko	どこ	Where?
dore	どれ	Which?
eiga	映画	movie
hai	はい	yes
iie	いいえ	no
ikitai	行きたい	want to go
mitai	見たい	want to see
romanchikku	ロマンチック	romantic
Sō desu ne.	そうですね。	Hmm, I wonder.
tabetai	食べたい	want to eat
terebi	テレビ	television

Letting Others Know What You Want

In this lesson you will learn to say what you would like to do and where you would like to go. This will allow you to move around freely in Japan. You will also learn some basic vocabulary related to Japanese food, clothing, and handicrafts.

Vocabulary

Useful Terms

ippin ryōri	一品料理	one-course meal; dishes a la carte
o-kanjō	お勘定	bill, check
teishoku	定食	main dish served with soup, rice, pickles, and salad; full-course lunch or dinner
washoku	和食	Japanese-style food

Food Terms

go-han	ご飯	cooked rice; meal
misoshiru	みそ汁	miso soup made from soybean paste
mizutaki	水炊き	simmered chicken, usually cooked at your table
nigirizushi	にぎり寿司	small rolls of cooked, vinegared rice with pieces of fresh seafood on top
awabi	あわび	abalone
ebi	えび	shrimp
ika	いか	squid, cuttlefish
ikura	いくら	salmon roe
maguro	まぐろ	tuna
tako	たこ	octopus
toro	とろ	belly flesh of tuna (considered a delicacy)
uni	うに	sea urchin
norimaki (**makizushi**)	のり巻き (巻きずし)	small rolls of rice with vegetables, wrapped in **nori** (tissue-thin seaweed)

okonomiyaki	お好み焼き	Japanese-style savory pancake containing vegetables, and other food stuff
o-sashimi	お刺身	slices of raw fish, served with soy sauce and wasabi (green horseradish)
o-sushi	お寿司	vinegared rice topped with raw fish or wrapped in **nori** (tissue-thin seaweed)
oyako donburi	親子丼	rice with chicken and eggs (**oyako** literally means "parents and children")
makunouchi teishoku	幕の内定食	variety of side dishes served with soup, rice, pickles, and salad; full-course lunch / dinner
rāmen	ラーメン	Chinese-style noodles in soup
shabushabu	しゃぶしゃぶ	simmered beef, usually cooked at the table
soba	そば	thin wheat noodles
sukiyaki	すき焼き	beef with vegetables, usually cooked at your table
takoyaki	たこ焼き	savory dumplings with octopus inside
tenpura	天ぷら	batter-dipped and deep-fried shrimp, fish and vegetables
teppan-yaki	鉄板焼き	meat and vegetables, usually cooked at your table on an iron grill
tonkatsu	トンカツ	pork cutlet
udon	うどん	thick wheat noodles
kitsune udon	きつね うどん	noodles with fried tōfu (bean curd)
tenpura udon	天ぷら うどん	noodles with tenpura
unajū	うな重	broiled marinated eels on cooked rice
yakitori	焼き鳥	charcoal-grilled chicken, chicken liver, and green onions on a bamboo stick

Drinks

agari (o-cha)	あがり （お茶）	Japanese green tea (This word is usually used only in sushi shops)
kōcha	紅茶	black tea
nomimono	飲み物	something to drink

o-cha	お茶	Japanese green tea (This word can be used anywhere.)
o-mizu	お水	water (This word can be used anywhere.)
o-sake	お酒	Japanese rice wine, sakē

Clothing

geta	下駄	wooden clogs
happi	はっぴ	happi coat (a colorful, waistlength coat)
jinbei	甚平	summertime Japanese-style casual wear
kimono	着物	kimono
obi	帯	sash worn with kimono
yukata	浴衣	summer cotton kimono
zōri	ぞうり	Japanese-style sandals

Entertainment

Bunraku	文楽	puppet play
eiga	映画	movie
Kabuki	歌舞伎	Kabuki play
Nō	能	Noh play

Art and Handicrafts

byōbu	屏風	folding screens
hanga	版画	woodblock print
katana	刀	sword
kokeshi	こけし	Japanese wooden doll
mingeihin	民芸品	folkcraft objects
sensu	扇子	paper folding fan
shinju	真珠	pearl
sumi-e	墨絵	brush painting
takeseihin (takezaiku)	竹製品 (竹細工)	bamboo craft objects, bamboo products
ukiyo-e	浮世絵	a particular genre of woodblock print
yakimono	焼物	pottery

Culture and vocabulary notes

The prefixes *go-* and *o-* in **go-han**, **o-sushi**, **o-cha**, **o-mizu**, and so on make the noun more polite to Japanese ears. Male speakers sometimes omit the prefixes, but female speakers almost always use them. In some cases, for example in **go-han**, the prefix cannot be dropped. You are advised to use only the polite form, which is always correct.

When a noun is used as the second part of a compound word, its pronunciation often changes slightly; e.g. in **nigirizushi** the *s* of **sushi** changes to *z*. The *ei* in **eiga** (movie) is pronounced more like *ē*, as are the *ei* spellings in other Japanese words

The word **o-cha** refers to Japanese green tea; **kōcha** (literally red tea) refers to black tea.

In English you "eat" soup, while in Japanese you "drink" soup. This reflects different eating habits. In the West, you use a soup spoon and do not lift the soup bowl. In Japan, you hold the bowl (usually a piece of lacquerware) in the palm of the left hand, bring the soup bowl close to your mouth, and drink or sip the soup. Any item in the soup such as fish, vegetables, or tofu may be eaten with the help of chopsticks. Good luck in picking up tofu with chopsticks; it requires some skill! And just as a note, when you pick up an item of food with chopsticks, it's not necessary to take it all in at one gulp. It's quite proper to bite off just a small piece.

Grammar

The next two sentence patterns will be of great help to you in restaurants, stores, and train stations. By mastering these patterns and the new verbs they introduce, you will be able to satisfy most of your basic needs as a traveler in Japan.

More detailed notes on verb conjugation will be presented later in this book. Looking at Sentence Patterns 2 and 3, however, we can make a few initial remarks about verbs and about Japanese sentence construction. First, note that stating the subject (I, in this case) is usually not necessary in Japanese when the subject is obvious from the context of the sentence. Also, **Tabetai desu** by itself is a complete sentence.

Sentence Pattern 2	
NOUN + **ga** / + VERB-INFINITIVE + **tai desu.** NOUN + が + VERB-INFINITIVE + たいです。	I'd like to + VERB + NOUN.

Examples

Sukiyaki ga tabetai desu.	I'd like to eat **sukiyaki**.
すき焼きが食べたいです。	
Biiru ga nomitai desu.	I'd like to drink beer.
ビールが飲みたいです。	
Kamera ga kaitai desu.	I'd like to buy a camera.
カメラが買いたいです。	
Kabuki ga mitai desu.	I'd like to see a Kabuki play.
歌舞伎が見たいです。	

Sentence Pattern 3

PLACE + **e** / ikitai desu.	I'd like to go to + place.
PLACE + へ行きたいです。	

Examples

Kyōto e ikitai desu.	I'd like to go to Kyoto.
京都へ行たいです。	
Nihon e ikitai desu.	I'd like to go to Japan.
日本へ行たいです。	

In Japanese, the words carrying a verbal meaning usually go at the very end of the sentence. In the previous examples, the -**tai desu** ending expresses the meaning "would like to do" and is attached to what we will call the verb-infinitive form of the verb. This will be explained later, but for now, memorize the following verb-infinitives and note the -**tai desu** endings.

eat	**tabe-**	**Tabetai desu.**	(I) would like to eat.
	食べ−	食べたいです。	
drink	**nomi-**	**Nomitai desu.**	(I) would like to drink.
	飲み−	飲みたいです。	
buy	**kai-**	**Kaitai desu.**	(I) would like to buy.
	買い−	買いたいです。	
see	**mi-**	**Mitai desu.**	(I) would like to see.
	見−	見たいです。	
go	**iki-**	**Ikitai desu.**	(I) would like to go.
	行き−	行きたいです。	

The word **desu** here has no real function other than to make the phrase sound more polite to Japanese ears (another use of **desu** in the sense of English "is" or "are" will be shown later). Thus, **Tabetai** means exactly the same thing as **Tabetai desu**, but it is more informal. Such informal expressions are most often used with family members or close friends. The matter is not so simple, however, and understanding when informal speech is appropriate requires more than a little knowledge of Japanese culture. A few informal forms are presented in this book because they are commonly used or show some important characteristics of Japanese words. But you are strongly advised to use only the polite forms of speech (including the **desu** in **Tabetai desu**, the **o-** in **o-sake**) until you become more familiar with the language and the people.

In Chapter 1 you learned the sentence pattern NOUN **o kudasai**, "Please give me NOUN," in which the noun (the item requested) was followed by the particle *o*. In Sentence Pattern 2 in this chapter, the particle *ga* is introduced as an object marker when the verb ends in **-tai desu**.

Biiru o kudasai. ビールをください。	Please give me a beer.
Biiru ga nomitai desu. ビールが飲みたいです。	I'd like to drink beer.

Among the younger generation in Japan, the particle **o** instead of **ga** is coming into use in the **-tai desu** construction. Whichever you may hear, the meaning is the same. Sentence Pattern 3 shows the particle **e**, which expresses direction or destination. It can be translated as "to," and follows the noun for the direction or destination.

Practice

1. Practice saying the following sentences aloud.

(a) to eat

O-sushi ga tabetai desu. お寿司が食べたいです。	I'd like to eat **sushi**.
Sukiyaki すき焼き	sukiyaki.
Tenpura 天ぷら	tenpura.

(b) to drink

Biiru ga nomitai desu.　　　　　　I'd like to drink beer.
ビールが飲みたいです。

Kōhii　　　　　　　　　　　　　　coffee.
こーひー

O-cha　　　　　　　　　　　　　　tea.
お茶

Sūpu　　　　　　　　　　　　　　soup.
スープ

(c) to buy

Kamera ga kaitai desu.　　　　　　I'd like to buy a camera.
カメラが買いたいです。

Rajio　　　　　　　　　　　　　　radio.
ラジオ

Shiidii　　　　　　　　　　　　　CD.
CD

Sūpu　　　　　　　　　　　　　　soup.
スープ

(d) to see

Bunraku ga mitai desu.　　　　　　I'd like to watch a puppet play.
文楽が見たいです。

Eiga　　　　　　　　　　　　　　a movie.
映画

Kabuki　　　　　　　　　　　　　a Kabuki play.
歌舞伎

Nō　　　　　　　　　　　　　　　a Noh play.
能

Terebi　　　　　　　　　　　　　television.
テレビ

(e) to go

Hokkaidō e ikitai desu.　　　　　　I'd like to go to Hokkaido.
北海道へ行きたいです。

Kyōto　　　　　　　　　　　　　Kyoto.
京都

Nihon (Nippon)   Japan.
日本 (ニッポン)

Ōsaka   Osaka.
大阪

Sapporo   Sapporo.
札幌

2. Practice Sentence Patterns 2 and 3 with the following words.

(a) to eat

biifustēki	sukiyaki	karē raisu	o-sushi
ビーフステーキ	すき焼き	カレーライス	お寿司

tenpura	o-sashimi	tonkatsu
天ぷら	お刺身	トンカツ

(b) to drink

biiru	o-mizu	kōhii
ビール	お水	コーヒー

orenjijūsu	o-cha	o-sake
オレンジジュース	お茶	お酒

(c) to buy

happi	obi	kamera
はっぴ	帯	カメラ

yukata	kimono	zōri
浴衣	着物	ぞうり

(d) to see

Bunraku	Kabuki	Nō	eiga
分楽	歌舞伎	能	映画

(e) to go

Hiroshima	Nara	Kōbe
広島	奈良	神戸

Tōkyō	Ōsaka	Okayama
東京	大阪	岡山

Nagasaki	Sapporo
長崎	札幌

Asking Questions and Saying "Yes"

So far you have been practicing statements. With these statements, you can express certain basic needs, but your ability to communicate is still limited. By learning to ask questions and answer them, you will be able to achieve real two-way communication.

Vocabulary

desu ka?	ですか？	is it?
ē	ええ	yes
hai	はい	yes

Culture and vocabulary notes

There are two common words for "yes" in Japanese: **hai** (はい) and **ē** (ええ). **Hai** is a little more formal than **ē**. **Hai** (but not **ē**) is also used to respond when someone calls out your name.

The particle **ka** used at the end of a sentence makes the sentence into a question. Notice that in forming questions in Japanese there is no inversion of word order as there is in English.

Grammar

Sentence Pattern 2A

NOUN + **ga** / + VERB-INFINITIVE + **tai desu ka?**	Would you like to +
NOUN + が + VERB-INFINITIVE + たいですか？	VERB + NOUN?

Examples

O-sushi ga tabetai desu ka?
お寿司が食べたいですか？ — Would you like to eat sushi?

O-sake ga nomitai desu ka?
お酒が飲みたいですか？ — Would you like to drink sake?

Kimono ga kaitai desu ka?
着物が買いたいですか？ — Would you like to buy a kimono?

Kabuki ga mitai desu ka?   Would you like to see a Kabuki play?
歌舞伎が見たいですか？

Sentence Pattern 3A	
PLACE + e / ikitai desu ka? PLACE + へ行きたいですか？	Would you like to go to + PLACE?

Examples

Nihon e ikitai desu ka?   Would you like to go to Japan?
日本へ行きたいですか？

Hawai e ikitai desu ka?   Would you like to go to Hawaii?
ハワイへ行きたいですか？

Sentence Pattern 4	
Hai (Ē), / + VERB-INFINITIVE + -tai desu. はい（ええ）、+ VERB-INFINITIVE + たいです。	Yes, I'd like to + VERB.

Examples

Hai (Ē), tabetai desu.   Yes, I'd like to eat (that).
はい（ええ）、食べたいです。

Hai (Ē), kaitai desu.   Yes, I'd like to buy (that).
はい（ええ）、買いたいです。

Hai (Ē), nomitai desu.   Yes, I'd like to drink (that).
はい（ええ）、飲みたいです。

Hai (Ē), mitai desu.   Yes, I'd like to see (that).
はい（ええ）、見たいです。

Hai (Ē), ikitai desu.   Yes, I'd like to go (there).
はい（ええ）、行きたいです。

Hai, tabetai desu is a complete sentence. You need not mention the object, which is usually understood from the context of the sentence. In English, this response often takes the form, "Yes, I'd like to." Notice that in Japanese an appropriate verb must always be used. **Hai, tabetai desu** is comparable to the English "Yes, I'd like to eat (it, some, this, etc.)."

Practice

Try translating the following sentences using the sentence patterns in this lesson. Turn to page 236 for the answers.

1. Would you like to eat sukiyaki?
   Yes, I'd like to eat some.
2. Would you like to drink a beer?
   Yes, I'd like to drink one.
3. Would you like to buy a camera?
   Yes, I'd like to buy one.
4. Would you like to watch television?
   Yes, I'd like to watch it.
5. Would you like to go to Japan?
   Yes, I'd like to go there.

Saying "No"

You practiced answering questions affirmatively in the previous lesson. Although negative answers are somewhat more complicated, it's important to learn them. You wouldn't want literally to be someone who can't say *no*.

Vocabulary

arimasen	ありません	does not exist
iie	いいえ	no

Grammar

Sentence Pattern 5

Iie / + VERB-INFINITIVE + **taku arimasen?**	No, I wouldn't like
いいえ + VERB-INFINITIVE + たくありません。	to + VERB.

Examples

Iie, tabetaku arimasen.
いいえ、食べたくありません。
No, I wouldn't like to eat that.

Iie, nomitaku arimasen.
いいえ、飲みたくありません。
No, I wouldn't like to drink that.

Iie, kaitaku arimasen.
いいえ、買いたくありません。
No, I wouldn't like to buy that.

Iie, mitaku arimasen.
いいえ、見たくありません。
No, I wouldn't like to see that.

In order to form the negative of the verb-form "would like to (do)," change the last letter *-i* in the affirmative *-tai* into *-ku* and add **arimasen**. Compare:

VERB-INFINITIVE + **-tai desu.**	**Tabetai desu.**	I would like
VERB-INFINITIVE + たいです。	食べたいです。	to eat.

VERB-INFINITIVE + **-taku arimasen.**	**Tabetaku arimasen**	I would not
VERB-INFINITIVE + たくありません。	食べたく	like to eat.
	ありません。	

Practice

Answer the following questions first with "yes" and then with "no."

1. Nihon e ikitai desu ka?
   日本へ行きたいですか？
2. Sukiyaki ga tabetai desu ka?
   すき焼きが食べたいですか？
3. Biiru ga nomitai desu ka?
   ビールが飲みたいですか？
4. Kimono ga kaitai desu ka?
   着物が買いたいですか？
5. Kyōto e ikitai desu ka?
   京都へ行きたいですか？
6. Eiga ga mitai desu ka?
   映画が見たいですか？
7. Kabuki ga mitai desu ka?
   歌舞伎が見たいですか？
8. Kamera ga kaitai desu ka?
   カメラが買いたいですか？
9. O-sake ga nomitai desu ka?
   お酒が飲みたいですか？
10. O-sushi ga tabetai desu ka?
    お寿司が食べたいですか？

Yes	No
1. Hai (Ē), ikitai desu. はい（えぇ）、行きたいです。	Iie, ikitaku arimasen. いいえ。いきたくありません。
2. Hai (Ē), tabetai desu. はい（えぇ）、食べたいです。	Iie, tabetaku arimasen. いいえ、食べたくありません。
3. Hai (Ē), nomitai desu. はい（えぇ）、飲みたいです。	Iie, nomitaku arimasen. いいえ、飲みたくありません。
4. Hai (Ē), kaitai desu. はい（えぇ）、買いたいです。	Iie, kaitaku arimasen. いいえ、買いたくありません。
5. Hai (Ē), ikitai desu. はい（えぇ）、行きたいです。	Iie, ikitaku arimasen. いいえ、行きたくありません。
6. Hai (Ē), mitai desu. はい（えぇ）、見たいです。	Iie, mitaku arimasen. いいえ、見たくありません。

7. Hai (Ē), mitai desu.   Iie, mitaku arimasen.
　はい（ええ）、見たいです。　　いいえ、見たくありません。

8. Hai (Ē), kaitai desu.   Iie, kaitaku arimasen.
　はい（ええ）、買いたいです。いいえ、買いたくありません。

9. Hai (Ē), nomitai desu.   Iie, nomitaku arimasen.
　はい（ええ）、飲みたいです。いいえ、飲みたくありません。

10. Hai (Ē), tabetai desu.   Iie, tabetaku arimasen.
　はい（ええ）、食べたいです。いいえ、食べたくありません。

Asking "What?" and "Which One?"

The next sentence pattern will enable you to ask "What would you like to (do)?" and "Which (one) would you like to (do)?"

Vocabulary

Dore?	どれ？	Which?
Dore to dore?	どれとどれ？	Which things? (plural)
Nani?	何？	What?
Nani to nani?	何と何？	What things? (plural)

Grammar

Sentence Pattern 2B

Nani ga / + verb-infinitive + -tai desu ka? 何が + verb-infinitive + たいですか？	What would you like to + verb?

Examples

Nani ga tabetai desu ka?
何が食べたいですか？
What would you like to eat?

Nani ga nomitai desu ka?
何が飲みたいですか？
What would you like to drink?

Nani ga kaitai desu ka?
何が買いたいですか？
What would you like to buy?

Nani ga mitai desu ka?
何が見たいですか？
What would you like to see?

Dore ga tabetai desu ka?
どれが食べたいですか？
Which one would you like to eat?

Dore ga nomitai desu ka?
どれが飲みたいですか？
Which one would you like to drink?

Dore ga kaitai desu ka?
どれが買いたいですか？
Which one would you like to buy?

Dore ga mitai desu ka?
どれが見たいですか？
Which one would you like to see?

The next sentence pattern is Sentence Pattern 2B with only a slight change. The literal translation of Sentence Pattern 2C is "What and what (or which and which) would you like to eat (drink, buy, etc.)?" This expression is rarely used in English but is often used in Japanese when the speaker wishes to ask if there is more than one thing that his listener would like to do or have. The number of items in the answer is not necessarily limited to two, even though the question here uses **nani** and *dore* twice only.

Sentence Pattern 2C	
Nani to nani ga / + VERB-INFINITIVE + **-tai desu ka?** 何 と 何 が + VERB-INFINITIVE + たいですか？	What things would you like to + VERB?
Dore to dore ga / + VERB-INFINITIVE + **-tai desu ka?** どれ と どれ が + VERB-INFINITIVE + たいですか？	Which things would you like to + VERB?

Example

Nani to nani ga tabetai desu ka?　　What things would you like to eat?
何 と 何 が 食べたいですか？

Nani to nani ga nomitai desu ka?　　What things would you like to drink?
何 と 何 が 飲みたいですか？

Nani to nani ga kaitai desu ka?　　What things would you like to buy?
何 と 何 が 買いたいですか？

Nani to nani ga mitai desu ka?　　What things would you like to see?
何 と 何 が 見たいですか？

Dore to dore ga tabetai desu ka?　　Which things would you like to eat?
どれ と どれ が 食べたいですか？

Dore to dore ga nomitai desu ka?　　Which things would you like to drink?
どれ と どれ が 飲みたいですか？

Dore to dore ga kaitai desu ka?　　Which things would you like to buy?
どれ と どれ が 買いたいですか？

Dore to dore ga mitai desu ka?　　Which things would you like to see?
どれ と どれ が 見たいですか？

Practice

1. Practice saying the following short dialogues aloud.

Nani ga tabetai desu ka?　　　　What would you like to eat?
何が食べたいですか？

O-sashimi ga tabetai desu.　　　　I'd like to eat **sashimi**.
お刺身が食べたいです。

Nani ga nomitai desu ka?　　　　What would you like to drink?
何が飲みたいですか？

Kōhii ga nomitai desu.　　　　I'd like to drink coffee.
コーヒーが飲みたいです。

Nani ga kaitai desu ka?　　　　What would you like to buy?
何が買いたいですか？

Kamera ga kaitai desu.　　　　I'd like to buy a camera.
カメラが買いたいです。

Nani ga mitai desu ka?　　　　What would you like to see?
何が見たいですか？

Kabuki ga mitai desu.　　　　I'd like to see a Kabuki play.
歌舞伎が見たいです。

Dore ga tabetai desu ka?　　　　Which one would you like to eat?
どれが食べたいですか？

Kore ga tabetai desu.　　　　I'd like to eat this.
これが食べたいです。

(pointing to an item on the menu or in the shop window)

Dore ga nomitai desu ka?　　　　Which one would you like to
どれが飲みたいですか？　　　　　drink?

Sore ga nomitai desu.　　　　I'd like to drink that.
それが飲みたいです。

(pointing to an item located near the listener)

Dore ga kaitai desu ka?　　　　Which one would you like to buy?
どれが買いたいですか？

Are ga kaitai desu.　　　　I'd like to buy that.
あれが買いたいです。

(pointing to an item away from both the speaker and the listener)

Dore ga mitai desu ka?
どれが見たいですか？

Which one would you like to see?

Kore ga mitai desu.
これが見たいです。

I'd like to see this one.

(pointing to an advertisement in the newspaper)

2. Practice saying the following dialogue aloud.

Nani to nani ga tabetai desu ka?
何と何が食べたいですか？

What (and what) would you like to eat?

Biifusutēki to sarada ga tabetai desu.
ビーフステーキとサラダが食べたいです。

I'd like to eat beefsteak and salad.

Nani to nani ga kaitai desu ka?
何と何が買いたいですか？

What (and what) would you like to buy?

Kimono to kamera to terebi ga kaitai desu.
着物とカメラとテレビが買いたいです。

I'd like to buy a kimono, a camera, and a television set.

Nani to nani ga mitai desu ka?
何と何が見たいですか？

What (and what) would you like to see?

Kabuki to Bunraku ga mitai desu.
歌舞伎と文楽が見たいです。

I'd like to see a Kabuki play and a puppet play.

3. Practice saying the following sentences aloud, substituting one word in each example.

Dore to dore ga tabetai desu ka? Which things would you like to eat?

              nomitai   drink?

              kaitai   buy?

              mitai   see?

どれとどれが食べたいですか？
　　　　飲みたい
　　　　買いたい
　　　　見たい

(Pointing to two items close to the speaker:)

Kore to kore ga tabetai desu.   I'd like to eat these (this and this).

nomitai	drink
kaitai	buy
mitai	see

これとこれが食べたいです。
　　　　　　飲みたい
　　　　　　買いたい
　　　　　　見たい

(Pointing to two items close to the listener:)

Sore to sore ga tabetai desu.   I'd like to eat those (that and that).

nomitai	drink
kaitai	buy
mitai	see

それとそれが食べたいです。
　　　　　　飲みたい
　　　　　　買いたい
　　　　　　見たい

(Pointing to two items at some distance from both the speaker and the listener:)

Are to are ga tabetai desu.   I'd like to eat those over there (that and that).

nomitai	drink
kaitai	buy
mitai	see

あれとこれが食べたいです。
　　　　　　飲みたい
　　　　　　買いたい
　　　　　　見たい

Asking "Where?"

In this lesson, you will learn an important sentence pattern that will allow to ask "Where do you want to go?" You will learn how to ask directions to a place in Lesson 11.

Vocabulary

Doko?	どこ	Where?
Doko to doko?	どことどこ？	To what places? (plural)

Grammar

Sentence Pattern 3B	
Doko e / ikitai desu ka? どこへ行きたいですか？	Where would you like to go?

Sentence Pattern 3C	
Doko to doko e / ikitai desu ka? どことどこへ行きたいで すか？	Where (and where) would you like to go? [or] To what places would you like to go?

As with **nani** and **dore**, the number of places in the answer need not be limited to two, although the question directly above uses **doko** twice only.

Practice

Practice these dialogues.

Doko e ikitai desu ka?
どこへ行きたいですか？

Where would you like to go?

Nihon e ikitai desu.
日本へ行きたいです。

I'd like to go to Japan.

Doko to doko e ikitai desu ka?
どことどこへ行きたいですか？

To what places would you like to go?

Kyōto to Nara e ikitai desu.
京都と奈良へ行きたいです。

I'd like to go to Kyoto and Nara.

Doko to doko e ikitai desu ka?
どことどこへ行きたいですか？

Where (and where) would you like to go?

Hiroshima to Miyajima e ikitai desu.
広島と宮島へ行きたいです。

I'd like to go to Hiroshima and Miyajima.

Eating at a Sushi Shop

Here you will review several of the sentence patterns and vocabulary that you
have learned in previous clessons.

Vocabulary

Irasshaimase!	いらっしゃいませ！	Welcome!
Konban wa. [or]	こんばんは。	Good evening.
Konnichi wa.	こんにちは。	Good afternoon.
o-kanjō	お勘定	the bill, the check

Culture and vocabulary notes

Instead of ordering a dish of sushi to be served at your table, it is sometimes
more fun to sit at the counter, order individual sushi as you wish, and watch the
skill with which it is made. Professional sushi makers are very proud of their
speed and dexterity. Before you enter, try to find out the price the shop charges,
since some shops are quite expensive.

You will hear the greeting **Irasshaimase!** every time you enter a shop or department store in Japan. It is simply a formal greeting of welcome from a shop-
keeper to a potential customer. No response is required from the customer.

Practice

Suppose a Japanese friend takes you out for sushi. The following will probably take place when you walk in the door and sit at the counter.

Sushi maker:

Irasshaimase!　　　　　　　　Welcome!
いらっしゃいませ！

You and your friend:

Konban wa.　　　　　　　　　Good evening.
こんばんは。

[or]　　　　　　　　　　　　　[or]

Konnichi wa.　　　　　　　　Good afternoon.
こんにちは。

Sushi maker:

Nani ni shimashō ka?　　　　What shall I make for you?
何にしましょうか？

Your friend (will turn to you and say):

Nani to nani ga tabetai desu ka?　What things would you like to eat?
何と何が食べたいですか？

Practice answers to your friend's question using the words under **nigirizushi** on page 33, such as the following.

Awabi ga tabetai desu.　　　I'd like to eat abalone.
あわびが食べたいです。

Uni to ikura ga tabetai desu.　I'd like to eat sea urchin and
うにといくらが食べたいです。　salmon roe.

Usually, if you go with a Japanese person, he or she will order for you. The sushi maker will then make two small **nigirizushi** of each kind ordered. If you go to the sushi shop by yourself, order the various types of **nigirizushi** in the following way:

Ika o kudasai.   Please give me squid.
いかをください。

Tako o kudasai.   Please give me octopus.
たこをください。

Maguro o kudasai.   Please give me tuna.
まぐろをください。

Awabi o kudasai.   Please give me abalone.
あわびをください。

If you don't know the name of the fish or prefer to pick whatever looks interesting from the case on the counter, just point to the item you want and say:

Sore o kudasai.   Please give me that.
それをください。

To order hot tea while you are eating, ask for **agari**.
Agari o kudasai.   Please give me some tea.
あがりをください。

When you have finished and are about to leave, ask for your bill as follows:
O-kanjō o kudasai.   May I have the bill, please?
お勘定をください。

Chapter 3

(Lessons 11 – 14)

Sentence Patterns Covered in Chapter 3	
Sentence Pattern 6	(Chotto sumimasen ga) / + PLACE + wa / doko desu ka? （ちょっとすみませんが）+ PLACE + はどこ ですか？
Sentence Pattern 7	NOUN OF DIRECTION + desu. NOUN OF DIRECTION + です。
Sentence Pattern 8	Kore wa / nan desu ka? これは何ですか？ Sore wa / nan desu ka? それは何ですか？ Are wa / nan desu ka? あれは何ですか？
Sentence Pattern 8A	Kore wa + NOUN + desu ka? これは + NOUN + ですか？ Sore wa + NOUN + desu ka? それは + NOUN + ですか？ Are wa + NOUN + desu ka? あれは + NOUN + ですか？
Sentence Pattern 8B	PERSON + wa / + PERSON + desu ka? PERSON + は + PERSON + ですか？ PERSON + no + PERSON + wa / + NOUN + desu ka? PERSON + の + PERSON + は + NOUN + ですか？

Sentence Pattern 9	Kore wa + NOUN + desu. これは + NOUN + です。 Sore wa + NOUN + desu. それは + NOUN + です。 Are wa + NOUN + desu. あれは + NOUN + です。
Sentence Pattern 10	Kore wa + NOUN + ja arimasen. これは + NOUN + じゃありません。 Kore wa + NOUN + de wa arimasen. これは + NOUN + ではありません。 Sore wa それは Are wa あれは
Sentence Pattern 11	Hai (Ē), / sō desu. はい（ええ）、そうです。
Sentence Pattern 12	Iie, / sō ja arimasen. いいえ、そうじゃありません。 Iie, / sō de wa arimasen. いいえ、そうではありません。

In Chapter 2 you were introduced to questions using the words **nani**, **dore**, and **doko**. In this chapter you will learn a series of related sentence patterns that will increase your ability to ask what, which, and where questions. You will learn how to ask directions, how to ask for information about the things you see around you on the street or in a restaurant, and how to discover more about the Japanese people with whom you will be spending some of your time.

Dialogue

ジョン ： ちょっとすみませんが、ホテルはどこですか？
浩　　： あそこです。
ジョン ： ホテルの中でレストランがありますか？
浩　　： はい、そうです。
ジョン ： あれはいいレストランですか？
浩　　： いいえ、そうじゃありません。悪いです。
ジョン ： それは何ですか？
浩　　： これはレストランじゃありません。郵便局です。
ジョン ： あれはいいレストランですか？
浩　　： あの中国料理のレストランですか？いいです。
ジョン ： あそこに行きたいですか？
浩　　： はい、行きたいです。

John	: Chotto sumimasen ga, hoteru wa doko desu ka?	Excuse me but where is the hotel?
Hiroshi	: Asoko desu.	It's over there.
John	: Hoteru no naka de resutoran ga arimasu ka?	Is there a restaurant inside the hotel?
Hiroshi	: Hai, sō desu.	Yes, there is.
John	: Are wa ii resutoran desu ka?	Is it a good restaurant?
Hiroshi	: Iie, so ja arimasen. Warui desu.	No, it's not (good). It's bad.
John	: Sore wa nan desu ka?	What's that (by you)?
Hiroshi	: Kore wa restoran ja arimasen. Yūbinkyoku desu.	This is not a restaurant. It's a post office.

John	: Are wa ii restoran desu ka?	Is that (over there) a good restaurant?
Hiroshi	: Ano Chūgoku ryōri no resutoran desu ka? Ii desu.	That Chinese restaurant over there? It's good.
John	: Asoko ni ikitai desu ka?	Do you want to go to that restaurant?
Hiroshi	: Hai, ikitai desu.	Yes, I want to go (there).

Dialogue vocabulary

arimasen	ありません	doesn't exist
arimasu ka?	ありますか？	does it exist?
asoko	あそこ	over there
chotto	ちょっと	a little
Chūgoku	中国	China
desu	です	is/are
desu ka?	ですか？	is/are there?
doko	どこ	Where?
hoteru	ホテル	hotel
ii	いい	good
naka	中	inside
ryōri	料理	food; cooking
Sō desu.	そうです。	It is./That's right.
sumimasen	すみません	excuse me

Culture and vocabulary notes

Chotto sumimasen ga is used like the English "Excuse me, but..." to make one's questioning of a stranger less abrupt. **Desu** was used earlier to make a sentence like **Tabetai desu** more polite. In this chapter, the meaning of **desu** is like that of the English "is" or "are."

Asking "Where?" and "Which Way?"

In this lesson you will learn how to ask directions. You will also learn the Japanese words for a variety of places and buildings.

Vocabulary

Amerika Ryōjikan	アメリカ領事館	American Consulate
Amerika Taishikan	アメリカ大使館	American Embassy
annaijo	案内所	information desk
apāto	アパート	apartment building
basu no noriba (basu no teiryūjo)	バスの乗り場 （バスの停留所）	bus stop
bijutsukan	美術館	art museum
biyōin	美容院	beauty salon
byōin	病院	hospital
chikatetsu no eki (chikatetsu no noriba)	地下鉄の駅 （地下鉄の乗り場）	subway station
daigaku	大学	university
eigakan	映画館	movie theater
eki	駅	station
eki no baiten	駅の売店	station store, kiosk
gakkō	学校	school
ginkō	銀行	bank
guriru	グリル	grill (in a Western-style hotel)
hikōjō, kūkō	飛行場、空港	airport
hoteru	ホテル	hotel (Western-style)
hoteru no shokudō	ホテルの食堂	hotel dining room
kippu uriba	切符売り場	ticket counter
kōban	交番	police substation
koin rokkā	コインロッカー	coin locker
kōshū denwa	公衆電話	public telephone
kusuriya (yakkyoku)	薬屋（薬局）	drugstore
nimotsu ichiji azukarijo	荷物一時預かり所	baggage check room

o-te'arai (toire)	お手洗い （トイレ）	toilet, bathroom
rihatsuten (sanpatsuya)	理髪店（散髪屋）	barber shop
ryokan	旅館	Japanese inn
shashin-ya	写真屋	photo studio
shokudō	食堂	dining room, eating place
takushii noriba	タクシー乗り場	taxi stand
toshokan	図書館	library
yūbinkyoku	郵便局	post office

Culture and vocabulary notes

Make sure you distinguish between **byōin** and **biyōin**. **Byōin** means "hospital" and **biyōin** means "beauty salon." In the names of hospitals, banks, and other institutions, the proper name, as in English, always comes first. For example: **Tōkyō-Mitsubishi Ginkō** (Tōkyō-Mitsubishi Bank).

The word **hikōjō** is a general word for "airport." The word **kūkō** is often used with the name of a specific airport, as in **Narita Kūkō** (Narita Airport). The suffix *-ya* as in **shashin-ya** or **hon-ya** means "shop" or "stand."

Like English, Japanese has many words for "toilet." Among these are **o-te'arai**, **toire** (borrowed from English), **o-benjo**, and **go-fujō**. **O-te'arai** is the safest, most general form for you to use. Instead of **rihatsuten**, the word **bābā shoppu** (from English "barber shop") is often used in Western-style hotels.

Grammar

If you have just arrived or are in a strange part of town, you can use the following sentence patterns to get your bearings, find a place to eat, or make your way home. **Dochira** means "which way?" Its meaning is similar to **doko** but is considered more polite and thus more appropriate to use with strangers.

Sentence Pattern 6

(Chotto sumimasen ga) PLACE + wa / doko desu ka? （ちょっとすみませんが）+ PLACE + はどこですか？	(Excuse me, but) where is + PLACE.
(Chotto sumimasen ga) / + PLACE + wa / dochira desu ka? （ちょっとすみませんが）+ PLACE + はどちらですか？	(Excuse me, but) which way is + PLACE?

Examples

(Chotto sumimasen ga) o-te'arai wa doko desu ka? （ちょっとすみませんが） お手洗いはどこですか？	(Excuse me, but) where is the toilet?
(Chotto sumimasen ga) Tōkyō Eki wa doko desu ka? （ちょっとすみませんが） 東京駅はどこですか？	(Excuse me, but) where is Tokyo Station?
(Chotto sumimasen ga) chikatetsu no eki wa dochira desu ka? （ちょっとすみませんが） 地下鉄の駅はどちらですか？	(Excuse me, but) which way is the subway station?
(Chotto sumimasen ga) kōshū denwa wa dochira desu ka? （ちょっとすみませんが） 公衆電話 はどちらですか？	(Excuse me, but) which way is a public telephone?

In Sentence Pattern 6 the particle used is *wa. Wa* has several uses in Japanese, but the one most frequently shown in this book is its use as a topic marker; that is, *wa* shows what you are talking or asking about. In Sentence Pattern 6, the topic of the sentence—that is, the noun followed by *wa*—corresponds to the subject in English.

Sentence Pattern 7	
NOUN OF DIRECTION + **desu.** NOUN OF DIRECTION + です。	It's + DIRECTION (here, this way, that way, etc.).

Examples

Koko desu. ここです。	It's here (by me).
Soko desu. そこです。	It's there (by you).
Asoko desu. あそこです。	It's over there.
Kochira (kotchi) desu. こちら（こっち）です。	It's this way.

Sochira (sotchi) desu.   It's near you.
そちら（そっち）です。
Achira (atchi) desu.   It's over that way.
あちら（あっち）です。

The new words in Sentence Pattern 7 are adverbial in English, but in Japanese they can be used as nouns or adverbs. Note the relationship of the following word groups: **kore, kono, koko, kochira (kotchi); sore, sono, soko, sochira (sotchi); are, ano, asoko, achira (atchi).** Pay particular attention to the variety of meanings given to words in the **sore** group throughout the translations in this book. The words **kotchi, sotchi,** and **atchi** are more informal than **kochira, sochira,** and **achira.**

Practice

1. (a) In a hotel. Practice repeating the following question, replacing the place each time.

(Chotto sumimasen ga)   (Excuse me, but)
  O-tearai wa doko desu ka?   Where is the toilet?
  Bā   bar?
  Rihatsuten   barber shop?
  Shokudō   dining room?
  Kōshū denwa   public telephone?
（ちょっとすみませんが）
  お手洗いはどこですか？
  バー
  理髪店
  食堂
  公衆電話

   (b) Practice giving answers to the above questions using the following expressions.

Koko desu.   It's here.
ここです。
Soko desu.   It's there.
そこです。
Asoko desu.   It's over there.
あそこです。

2. (a) In Tokyo. Practice repeating the following question, replacing the place each time.

(Chotto sumimasen ga)	(Excuse me, but) which way is the
Amerika Taishikan wa dochira desu ka?	American Embassy?
Ginkō	bank?
Basu no noriba	bus stop?
Kusuriya	drugstore?
Byōin	hospital?

（ちょっとすみませんが）アメリカ大使館はどちらですか？
銀行
バスの乗り場
薬屋
病院

(b) Practice answering the above questions using the following expressions.

Kochira desu.　　It's this way.
こちらです。

Sochira desu.　　It's that way (toward the listener).
そちらです。

Achira desu.　　It's over that way.
あちらです。

3. At a train station. Practice saying the following short dialogues aloud.

Chotto sumimasen ga, nimotsu ichiji azukarijo wa doko desu ka?　　Excuse me, but where is the baggage check room?
ちょっとすみませんが、
荷物一時預かり所はどこですか？

Asoko desu.　　It's over there.
あそこです。

Chotto sumimasen ga, annaijo wa doko desu ka?　　Excuse me, but where is the information desk?
ちょっとすみませんが、案内所は
どこですか？

Soko desu.　　It's there (by you).
そこです。

Chotto sumimasen ga, eki no baiten
  wa dochira desu ka?
ちょっとすみませんが、駅の売店
  はどちらですか？

Excuse me, but where is the
  station store?

Achira desu.
あちらです。

It's over that way.

Chotto sumimasen ga, kippu uriba wa
  dochira desu ka?
ちょっとすみませんが、切符売り
  場はどちらですか？

Excuse me, but which way is
  the ticket counter?

Sochira desu.
そちらです。

It's there, in your direction.

Chotto sumimasen ga, takushii noriba wa
  dochira desu ka?
ちょっとすみませんが、タクシー
  乗り場はどちらですか？

Excuse me, but which way is
  the taxi stand?

Kochira desu.
こちらです。

It's this way.

4. Translate the following sentences into Japanese. Turn to page 236 for answers.

  (a) Excuse me, but which way is the movie theater?

  (b) Excuse me, but where is the police substation?

  (c) Excuse me, but which way is the post office?

  (d) Excuse me, but where is the train station?

  (e) Excuse me, but which way is Tokyo Station?

  (f) Excuse me, but which way is the subway station?

  (g) Excuse me, but where is the taxi stand?

  (h) Excuse me, but where is the beauty salon?

· LESSON 12 ·

Asking What it is When You Don't Know

In this lesson you will learn how to ask questions about the identity of places and things and how to answer such questions. You will also learn the names of a number of famous places in Japan.

Vocabulary

Ashino-ko	芦ノ湖	Lake Ashino
Biwa-ko	琵琶湖	Lake Biwa
Fuji-san	富士山	Mt Fuji
Ise Jingū	伊勢神宮	Grand Shrine of Ise
Kokkai Gijidō	国会議事堂	National Diet Building
Kyōto Daigaku (Kyōdai)	京都大学 (京大)	Kyoto University
Kōkyo (or Gōsho)	皇居 (御所)	Imperial Palace
Nihon-kai	日本海	Japan Sea
Nijō-jō	二条城	Nijo Castle
Ōsaka-jō	大阪城	Osaka Castle
Ryōan-ji	竜安寺	Ryoan Temple
Setonai-kai	瀬戸内海	Inland Sea
Sumiyoshi Taisha	住吉大社	Sumiyoshi Shrine
Tōkyō Daigaku (Tōdai)	東京大学 (東大)	Tokyo University

Culture and vocabulary notes

The suffix **-dai** is short for **daigaku**, which means "university." The **Kyō-** in **Kyōdai** and the **Tō-** in **Tōdai** are contracted forms of **Kyōto** and **Tōkyō**, respectively. **Jingū** means "grand shrine," and **jinja** means "shrine." Other suffixes used in the vocabulary list are as follows:

-ji	寺	temple	-ko	湖	lake
-jō	城	castle	-san	山	mountain
-kai	海	sea			

Grammar

If you're interested in architecture, handicrafts, or just identifying the things around you, the next two sentence patterns will help you get the answers that will satisfy your curiosity.

Notice again that Japanese normally makes no distinction between singular and plural. In the sentence patterns below, the words **kore**, **sore**, and **are** can refer to one object, to a group of similar objects, or to a group of different objects. The context should make the intended meaning clear. In these patterns, **desu** functions like "is" or "are" in English.

Sentence Pattern 8

Kore wa / nan desu ka? これは何ですか？	What is this?
Sore wa / nan desu ka? それは何ですか？	What is that (by you)?
Are wa / nan desu ka? あれは何ですか？	What is that (over there)?

Sentence Pattern 9

Kore wa / + NOUN + desu. これは + NOUN + です	This is (These are) + NOUN.
Sore wa / + NOUN + desu. それは + NOUN + です。	That (by you) is (They are) + NOUN.
Are wa / + NOUN + desu. あれは + NOUN + です。	That (over there) is (Those are) + NOUN.

Examples

Kore wa Kyōto Daigaku desu.
これは京都大学です。
This is Kyoto University.

Sore wa Setonai-kai desu.
それは 瀬戸内海 です。
That (what you are referring to) is the Inland Sea.

Are wa Fuji-san desu.
あれは富士山です。
That (over there) is Mt. Fuji.

In Chapter 2 you learned the word **nani** for "what." **Nan** is used instead of **nani** before a word beginning with *d*.

Either **nan** or **nani** can be used before a word beginning with *t* or *n*. Before other consonants or vowels, only **nani** is used.

Kore wa nan desu ka?	What is this?
これは何ですか。	
Nan to nani ga tabetai desu ka?	What things do you want to eat?
何と何が食べたいですか。	

Practice

1. On a street. Practice saying the following short dialogues aloud.

(a) Pointing to a giant paper carp (**koinobori**) flying from a pole next to a house:

Are wa nan desu ka?	What is that?
あれは何ですか？	
Are wa koinobori desu.	That's a **koinobori**.
あれは鯉のぼりです。	

(b) Pointing to a shrine:

Are wa nan desu ka?	What is that?
あれは何ですか？	
Are wa jinja desu.	That's a shrine.
あれは神社です。	

(c) Looking at the small strips of paper tied onto a tree near the shrine (**o-mikuji**):

Are wa nan desu ka?	What are those?
あれは何ですか？	
Are wa o-mikuji desu.	Those are **o-mikuji**.
あれはおみくじです。	

(d) Pointing to a large cluster of buildings:

Are wa nan desu ka?	What is that place over there?
あれは何ですか？	
Are wa Tōdai desu.	That's Tokyo University.
あれは東大です。	

Culture and vocabulary notes

Koinobori are giant paper or cloth carp flown from poles next to houses during the celebration of Children's Day (May 5th). The carp is a symbol of strength and perseverance. **O-mikuji** are written paper fortunes that you can select after paying a small amount of money at a temple or a shrine. After reading your fortune, you fold it and attach it to a branch of a tree to bring good luck. Shrines, by the way, are Shintō and temples are Buddhist. Most Japanese practice both religions.

2. In a restaurant. Practice saying the following short dialogues aloud.
   (a) Pointing to the white cubes in your soup:

   Kore wa nan desu ka?   What are these?
   これは何ですか？

   Sore wa tōfu desu.   That's tofu.
   それは豆腐です。

   (b) Pointing to an item on the counter of a sushi shop:

   Kore wa nan desu ka?   What is this?
   これは何ですか。

   Kore wa uni desu.   This is sea urchin.
   これはうにです。

   (c) Pointing to your friend's drink:

   Sore wa nan desu ka?   What is that?
   それは何ですか？

   Kore wa remonēdo desu.   This is lemonade.
   これはレモネードです。

   (d) Pointing to what is being served at another table:

   Are wa nan desu ka?   What's that over there?
   あれは何ですか？

   Are wa makunouchi teishoku desu.   That's full-course lunch / dinner.
   あれは幕の内定食です。

Finding Out What It Is (and Isn't)

In this lesson you will learn to ask whether you have correctly identified a person, place, or object. You will also learn how to say to another person that they have incorrectly identified a person, place, or object.

Vocabulary

hon-ya	本屋	bookstore
kissaten	喫茶店	coffee shop
manga	漫画	comic book
Sō desu.	そうです。	It is. (They are.)
Sō dewa arimasen.	そうではありません。	It isn't. (They aren't.) (Formal)
Sō ja arimasen.	そうじゃありません。	It isn't. (They aren't.) (Informal)

Grammar

Look again at Sentence Patterns 8 and 9 in Lesson 12 and compare them with the two that are shown below.

Sentence Pattern 8A

Kore wa / + NOUN + desu ka? これは + NOUN + ですか？	Is this + NOUN?
Sore wa / + NOUN + desu ka? それは + NOUN + ですか？	Is that (by you) + NOUN?
Are wa / + NOUN + desu ka? あれは + NOUN + ですか？	Is that (over there) + NOUN?

Examples

Kore wa Shinjuku Eki desu ka?　　Is this Shinjuku Station?
これは新軸駅ですか？

Sore wa manga desu ka?　　Are they (what you have) comic books?
それは漫画ですか？

Are wa kissaten desu ka?   Is that (over there) a coffee shop?
これは喫茶店ですか？

To express the negative, use **ja arimasen** (a bit informal) or **de wa arimasen** (more polite) after the noun. Compare:

Kore wa hon-ya desu.   This is a book store.
これは本屋です。

Kore wa hon-ya ja arimasen. (informal) This is not a book store.
これは本屋じゃありません。

Kore wa hon-ya de wa arimasen. (formal) This is not a book store.
これは本屋ではありません。

Sentence Pattern 10	
Kore wa / + NOUN + **ja arimasen.** これは + NOUN + じゃありません。	This isn't + NOUN.
Kore wa / + NOUN + **de wa arimasen.** これは + NOUN + ではありません。	
Sore wa それは	That (by you)
Are wa あれは	That (over there)

Examples

Kore wa yūbinkyoku ja arimasen.   This isn't a post office.
これは郵便局じゃありません。

Sore wa ginkō ja arimasen.   That (by you) isn't a bank.
それは銀行じゃありません。

Are wa Tanaka-san ja arimasen.   That (over there) isn't Mr Tanaka.
あれは田中さんじゃありません。

Review the expansion of some of the patterns you have learned in this lesson.

S.P. 8: Kore wa nan desu ka?   What is this?
         これはなんですか？

S.P. 9: Kore wa yūbinkyoku desu.   This is a post office.
         これは郵便局です。

S.P. 8A: Kore wa yūbinkyoku desu ka? 　　　　Is this a post office?
　　　　これは郵便局ですか？

S.P. 10: Kore wa yūbinkyoku ja arimasen. 　　This is not a post office.
　　　　これは郵便局じゃありません。

The affirmative **Kore wa yūbinkyoku desu** and the negative **Kore wa yūbinkyoku ja arimasen** can be used to respond to the question **Kore wa yūbinkyoku desu ka?** by using the words **hai (ē)** or **iie** that you have already learned. Recall:

Unagi ga tabetai desu ka? 　　　　Would you like to eat eel?
うなぎが食べたいですか？

Hai, tabetai desu. [or] 　　　　Yes, I'd like to eat that. [or]
はい、食べたいです。

Iie, tabetaku arimasen. 　　　　No, I wouldn't like to eat that.
いいえ、食べたくありません。

Now, using the patterns in this chapter:

Kore wa yūbinkyoku desu ka? 　　　　Is this a post office?
これは郵便局ですか？

Hai, (kore wa) yūbinkyoku desu. 　　Yes, this is a post office.
はい、（これは）郵便局です。 　　　　[or]
[or]

Iie, (kore wa) yūbinkyoku ja arimasen. 　No, this is not a post office.
いいえ、（これは）郵便局じゃありません。

The topic **kore wa** is optional in the answer since it is usually understood from the context of the situation.

When asked a question like "Is this the post office?" it is usually unnecessary to repeat the noun in question when answering, just as in English when we say "Yes, it is," or "No, it isn't." The following sentence patterns show the comparable short responses in Japanese.

Sentence Pattern 11	
Hai (Ē), / sō desu. はい（ええ）、そうです。	Yes, it is (they are).

Sentence Pattern 12

Iie, / sō ja arimasen. いいえ、そうじゃありません。	No, it isn't (they aren't). (Informal)
Iie, / so de wa arimasen. いいえ、そうではありません。	No, it isn't (they aren't). (Formal)

Examples

Kore wa ginkō desu ka?   Is this a bank?
これは銀行ですか？

Hai, sō desu.   Yes, it is.
はい、そうです。

Iie, sō ja arimasen.   No, it isn't.
いいえ、そうじゃありません。

Are wa unagi desu ka?   Is that eel?
これはうなぎですか？

Hai, sō desu.   Yes, it is.
はい、そうです。

Iie, sō ja arimasen.   No, it isn't.
いいえ、そうじゃありません。

Practice

1. Give affirmative and negative responses to each of these questions. Turn to page 236 for answers.

    (a) Kore wa yūbinkyoku desu ka?   Is this a post office?
    これは郵便局ですか？

    (b) Are wa unagi desu ka?   Are those eels?
    これはうなぎですか？

    (c) Sore wa tōfu desu ka?   Is that (which you are eating) tofu?
    それは豆腐ですか？

    (d) Are wa jinja desu ka?   Is that a shrine?
    あれは神社ですか？

    (e) Kore wa Shinjuku Eki desu ka?   Is this Shinjuku Station?
    これは新宿駅ですか？

(f) Are wa Tōdai desu ka?   Is that Tokyo University?
あれは東大ですか？

(g) Kore wa basu no noriba desu ka?   Is this the bus stop?
これはバスの乗り場ですか？

2. Use the short responses in Sentence Patterns 11 and 12 to give affirmative
    and negative answers to the practice questions in #1 above.

Asking about the Family

In this lesson you will learn various terms for family members. These terms are different, depending on whether you are talking about a member of your own family or someone else's family. You will also learn the names for various occupations and how to ask questions to find out more about other people and their families.

Vocabulary
Kinship Terms

When Talking About Your Own Family:	When Talking About Someone Else's Family:	Meaning
chichi 父	o-tō-san お父さん	father
haha 母	o-kā-san お母さん	mother
kodomo 子ども	o-ko-san お子さん	child
musuko 息子	musuko-san 息子さん	son
musume 娘	musume-san (o-jō-san) 娘さん（お嬢さん）	daughter
tsuma 妻	oku-san 奥さん	wife
shujin 主人	go-shujin ご主人	husband

Personal Pronouns

anata	あなた	you
kare	彼	he
kanojo	彼女	she
watakushi	私	I (polite)

Nationalities

Amerikajin	アメリカ人	American (person)
Furansujin	フランス人	French
Hawaijin	ハワイ人	Hawaiian
Igirisujin	イギリス人	English
Itariajin	イタリア人	Italian
Kanadajin	カナダ人	Canadian
Nihonjin	日本人	Japanese
Ōsutorariajin	オーストラリア人	Australian
Supeinjin	スペイン人	Spanish

Occupations

bijinesuman	ビジネスマン	businessman
eki-in	駅員	station employee
gakusei	学生	student
ginkō-in	銀行員	bank employee
haisha	歯医者	dentist
hisho	秘書	secretary
hosutesu	ホステス	hostess (in a bar or cabaret)
isha (o-isha-san)	医者 （お医者さん）	medical doctor
kangofu	看護婦	nurse
keikan (o-mawari-san)	警官 （おまわりさん）	policeman
kōkanshu (denwa no kokanshu)	交換手 （電話の交換手）	telephone operator
sarariiman	サラリーマン	white-collar employee
sensei	先生	teacher
shachō	社長	company president
shashō	車掌	train or bus conductor
ten-in	店員	store clerk
untenshu	運転手	driver

Culture and vocabulary notes

In the list above, kinship terms are divided into two groups. The first group is used when you refer to those in your own family. The next group shows terms of respect used when you refer to or ask about those in another person's family. The Japanese are very observant of this distinction. When addressing his own father or mother directly, however, a Japanese person will use **o-tō-san** or **o-kā-san** to show respect. When directly addressing his son or daughter, a Japanese will usually use the personal name rather than the kinship term. A more complete list of these kinship terms appears in Appendix 1.

Japanese also have several other words for "I" and "you," but since their correct usage requires considerable familiarity with Japanese social structure, you are advised to stick to **watakushi** for yourself and **anata** (or, preferably, the family name with the suffix -**san**) for the person with whom you are speaking. The following alternate forms are provided, since you will probably hear them often.

boku	僕	I	male speaker, informal
ore	俺	I	male speaker, very informal
watashi	私	I	a bit more informal than **watakushi**
kimi	君	you	male speaker, informal
o-mae	お前	you	for children and inferiors
o-taku	おたく	you	polite

The Japanese are much more comfortable using the family name + -**san** than they are using such words as **kare**, **kanojo**, and **anata**. The suffix -**san** can mean "Mr.," "Mrs.," "Miss," or "Ms.," but you needn't think of it as stuffy or too formal. The suffix -**chan** is often attached to children's first names: **Kazuko-chan**, **Mieko-chan**, **Ken-chan**, etc.

When addressing or referring to teachers or doctors, the word **sensei** is used after the family name: **Satō Sensei**, **Yamamoto Sensei**, etc. **O-isha-san** and **o-mawari-san** can be used to address doctors and policemen instead of the name plus **sensei** or -**san**. NEVER use -**san** with your own name.

Grammar

Use the following sentence pattern to find out more about the people with whom you are speaking and their families.

Sentence Pattern 8B	
PERSON + **wa** / + PERSON + **desu ka?** PERSON + は + PERSON + ですか？	Is + PERSON + a + NOUN?
PERSON + **no** + PERSON + **wa** / + **desu ka?** PERSON + の + PERSON + は + NOUN+ ですか？	Is + PERSON + (of PERSON) + a NOUN?

Examples

Tanaka-san wa Nihonjin desu ka?	Is Mr. (Mrs., etc.) Tanaka Japanese?
田中さんは日本人ですか？	
Oku-san wa o-isha-san desu ka?	Is your wife a doctor?
奥さんはお医者さんですか？	
Tanaka-san no o-tō-san wa sarariiman desu ka?	Is Mr. Tanaka's father a white-collar employee?
田中さんのお父さんはサラリーマンですか？	
O-tō-san no oku-san wa Amerikajin desu ka?	Is your father's wife an American?
お父さんの奥さんはアメリカ人ですか？	

Sentence Pattern 8B is merely an expansion of the patterns you have learned in this chapter. An important addition, though, is the particle **no** to indicate that the following noun "belongs" to the preceding one. Thus, **Tanaka-san no o-tō-san** means "Mr Tanaka's father," and **Otō-san no oku-san** means "your father's wife." Notice that because Japanese has two distinct vocabularies for family relationships, **anata no** in a phrase like **anata no oku-san** (your wife) would be redundant.

When answering a question like **Tanaka-san wa Nihonjin desu ka?** the affirmative short response, **Hai, sō desu**, is perfectly appropriate. The negative short response, **Iie, sō ja arimasen**, is also correct, but usually you want to give a bit more information to clarify your answer.

Tanaka-san wa Nihonjin desu ka?	Is Mr Tanaka a Japanese (citizen)?
田中さんは日本人ですか？	
Hai, (Tanaka-san wa) Nihonjin desu. [or] **Hai, sō desu.**	Yes, Mr Tanaka is a Japanese. [or] Yes, that's right.
はい、（田中さんは）日本人です。[or] はい、そうです。	
[or]	[or]
Iie, (Tanaka-san wa) Nihonjin ja arimasen. Amerikajin desu.	No, Mr Tanaka is not a Japanese. He's an American.
いいえ、（田中さんは）日本人じゃありません。アメリカ人です。	

[or]
Iie, sō ja arimasen. Amerikajin desu.
いいえ、そうじゃありません。
　アメリカ人です。

No, that's not correct.
　He's an American.

Oku-san wa hisho desu ka?
奥さんは秘書ですか？

Is your wife a secretary?

Hai, sō desu.
はい、そうです。

Yes, she is.

**Iie, (tsuma wa) hisho ja arimasen.
　Isha desu.**
いいえ、（妻は）秘書じゃあ
　りません。医者です。

No, my wife (is not a secretary. She)
　is a doctor.

[or]
Iie, sō ja arimasen. Isha desu.
いいえ、そうじゃありません。
　医者です。

[or]
No, that's not correct. She's a doctor.

[or]
Iie, isha desu.
いいえ、医者です。

[or]
No, she's a doctor.

Practice

1. Answer in the affirmative.

　Anata wa Amerikajin desu ka?
　あなたはアメリカ人ですか？

Are you an American?

　Hai, sō desu.
　はい、そうです。

Yes, I am.

　O-ko-san wa gakusei desu ka?
　お子さんは学生ですか？

Is your son (or daughter)
　a student?

　Hai, sō desu.
　はい、そうです。

Yes, he (or she) is.

　Musume-san wa ginkōin desu ka?
　娘さんは銀行員ですか？

Is your daughter a bank
　employee?

　Hai, sō desu.
　はい、そうです。

Yes, she is.

2. Answer in the negative.

Anata wa sensei desu ka?
あなたは先生ですか？

Are you a teacher?

Iie. (Sensei ja arimasen.)
いいえ。（先生じゃありません。）

No. (I'm not a teacher.)

Gakusei desu.
学生です。

I'm a student.

Tanaka-san wa keikan desu ka?
田中さんは警官ですか？

Is Mr Tanaka a policeman?

Iie. (Keikan ja arimasen.) Untenshu desu.
いいえ。（警官じゃありません。）
運転手です。

No. (He is not a policeman.)
He's a driver.

Oku-san wa hisho desu ka?
奥さんは秘書ですか？

Is your wife a secretary?

Iie. (Hisho ja arimasen.) Ten-in desu.
いいえ。（秘書じゃありません。）
店員です。

No. (She is not a secretary.)
She's a clerk.

3. Answer in the negative.

Tanaka-san no o-tō-san wa haisha desu ka?
田中さんのお父さんは歯医者ですか？

Is Mr Tanaka's father
a dentist?

Iie, (Tanaka-san no o-tō-san wa) sensei desu.
いいえ。（田中さんのお父さんは）
先生です。

No, (Mr Tanaka's
father is) a teacher.

Musuko-san wa gakusei desu ka?
息子さんは学生ですか？

Is your son a student?

Iie, (musuko wa) sarariiman desu.
いいえ。（息子は）サラリーマンです。

No, (my son is) a white-
collar employee.

Chapter 4

(Lessons 15 – 16)

Sentence Patterns Covered in Chapter 4	
Sentence Pattern 13	VERB-INFINITIVE + -**mashō.** VERB-INFINITIVE + ましょう。
Sentence Pattern 14	NOUN + o / + VERB-INFINITIVE + -**mashō.** NOUN + を + VERB-INFINITIVE + ましょう。
Sentence Pattern 14A	NOUN + o / + VERB-INFINITIVE + -**mashō ka?** NOUN + を + VERB-INFINITIVE + ましょうか？
Sentence Pattern 14B	**Nani o** / + VERB-INFINITIVE + -**mashō ka?** 何を + VERB-INFINITIVE + ましょうか？ **Dore o** / + VERB-INFINITIVE + -**mashō ka?** どれを + NOUN + ましょうか？
Sentence Pattern 15	PLACE + e / + **ikimashō.** PLACE + へ行きましょう。
Sentence Pattern 15A	PLACE [OR] NOUN + e / **ikimashō ka?** PLACE / NOUN + へ行きましょうか？
Sentence Pattern 15B	**Doko e** / **ikimashō ka?** どこへ行きましょうか？

Now that you have learned how to get your bearings and how to express your needs in Japanese, it's time to begin thinking of "we" as well as "I." After all, so many things are more fun when the experience is shared. In this chapter you will learn to make suggestions to and ask advice from your Japanese friends about the things you can do together—trips, sports, shopping, eating, enjoying.

Dialogue

圭子 ： 今晩,何がしたいですか？
由美 ： カラオケをしましょう！
圭子 ： そうしましょう。
由美 ： ごはんは何を食べたいですか？
圭子 ： お寿司を食べましょう。
由美 ： どこへ行きましょうか？
圭子 ： 「桜寿司」に行きましょう。
由美 ： あそこはおいしいですね。そうしましょう。
　　　　 そして、ちょっと買い物をしましょうか？
圭子 ： 洋服を買いましょう。
由美 ： じゃあ、出かけましょう。

Keiko :	**Konban, nani ga shitai desu ka?**	What do you want to do tonight?
Yumi :	**Karaoke o shimashō.**	Let's do karaoke!
Keiko :	**Sō shimashō.**	Okay, let's do it!
Yumi :	**Go-han wa nani o tabetai desu ka?**	What do you want to eat for dinner?
Keiko :	**O-sushi o tabemashō.**	Let's eat sushi.
Yumi :	**Doko e ikimashō ka?**	Where shall we go (to eat)?
Keiko :	**"Sakura Sushi" ni ikimashō.**	Let's go to "Sakura Sushi."
Yumi :	**Asoko wa oishii desu ne. Sō shimashō.**	Oh, that place is delicious. Let's do it!
	Soshite, chotto kaimono o shimashō ka?	And also shall we do a little shopping?
Keiko :	**Yōfuku o kaimashō.**	Let's buy some clothes!
Yumi :	**Jā, dekakemashō.**	Okay, let's go out (now).

Dialogue vocabulary

dekakemashō	出かけましょう	Let's go out.
ikimashō	行きましょう	Let's go.
kaimashō	買いましょう	Let's buy (it).
kaimono	買い物	shopping
karaoke	カラオケ	karaoke singing
konban	今晩	This evening
jā	じゃあ	Okay/Well then
oishii	おいしい	delicious
shimashō	しましょう	Let's do (it).
soshite	そして	And also/And then …
tabemashō	食べましょう	Let's eat.
yōfuku	洋服	clothes

Making Suggestions

In this lesson you will learn how to propose an action (Let's do …) to someone. You will also learn the Japanese words for a variety of sports and other activities.

Vocabulary

shimashō	しましょう	Let's do (it).

Sports and Games:

bōringu	ボーリング	bowling
dansu	ダンス	dancing
gorufu	ゴルフ	golf
sukēto	スケート	skating
sukii	スキー	skiing
tenisu	テニス	tennis

Other Activities

benkyō	勉強	study
kankō	観光	sightseeing
kekkon	結婚	marriage
renshū	練習	practice
ryokō	旅行	travel, trip
sanpo	散歩	a walk
shokuji	食事	meal

Culture and vocabulary notes

Many modern sports and activities use loanwords and so are written in katakana. Of course, traditional Japanese sports and activities, such as **karate** (空手), **ikebana** (生け花), **jūdo** (寿度), and tea ceremony (**chanoyu**) (茶の湯) are written either solely in kanji or in a combination of kanji and hiragana.

You will often hear Japanese people use the exclamatory word **ne** at the end of a sentence or phrase. It is usually used, as in the dialogue, by a speaker as a way of inviting the listener's agreement. It may also show the speaker's agreement with what has just been said by another person, or to show that the speaker is following the flow of the conversation. It is similar to the English "isn't it?" or "aren't you?" but is used much more often. The frequently used expression "**Sō desu ne.**" can usually be translated as "That's right" or "I see," but may also indicate that the speaker is thinking things over if pronounced with uncertainty.

Grammar

Sentence Pattern 13	
VERB-INFINITIVE + -**mashō.** VERB-INFINITIVE + ましょう。	Let's + VERB.

Examples

Iki- + -**masho** → **Ikimashō.**   Let's go.
行き＋ましょう→行きましょう。

Kai- + -**mashō** → **Kaimashō.**   Let's buy.
買い＋ましょう→買いましょう。

Mi- + -**mashō** → **Mimashō.**   Let's see. (Let's watch.)
見＋ましょう→見ましょう。

Nomi- + -**mashō** → **Nomimashō.**   Let's drink.
飲み＋ましょう→飲みましょう。

Shi- + -**mashō** → **Shimashō.**   Let's do (it).
し＋ましょう→しましょう。

Tabe- + -**masho** → **Tabemashō.**   Let's eat.
食べ＋ましょう→食べましょう。

The sentence pattern VERB-INFINITIVE + -**mashō** is used to propose an action to someone else. Compare this with the pattern you learned in Chapter 2 that meant "I would like to VERB": VERB-INFINITIVE + -**tai desu**. Note that even in the absence of a subject or object, both are complete sentences.

Ikitai desu.   **Ikimashō.**
行きたいです。   行きましょう。

Kaitai desu.   **Kaimashō.**
買いたいです。   買いましょう。

Mitai desu.   **Mimashō.**
見たいです。   見ましょう。

Nomitai desu.	Nomimashō.
飲みたいです。	飲みましょう。
Tabetai desu.	Tabemashō.
食べたいです。	食べましょう。
Shitai desu.	Shimashō.
したいです。	しましょう。

The following two sentence patterns are Sentence Pattern 13 plus a noun that shows what it is you are suggesting.

Sentence Pattern 14

NOUN + **o** / + VERB-INFINITIVE + **-mashō.**	Let's + VERB + NOUN.
NOUN + を VERB-INFINITIVE + ましょう。	

Examples

Sukiyaki o tabemashō.	Let's eat sukiyaki.
すき焼きを食べましょう。	
O-sake o nomimashō.	Let's drink sake.
お酒を飲みましょう。	
Kabuki o mimashō.	Let's see a Kabuki play.
歌舞伎を見ましょう。	
Gorufu o shimashō.	Let's play golf.
ゴルフをしましょう。	
Kimono o kaimashō.	Let's buy a kimono.
着物を買いましょう。	

Sentence Pattern 15

PLACE + **e** / ikimashō.	Let's go to + PLACE.
PLACE + へ行きましょう。	

Examples

Yokohama e ikimashō.	Let's go to Yokohama.
横浜へ行きましょう。	
Eiga e ikimashō.	Let's go to a movie.
映画へ行きましょう。	
O-sushiya e ikimashō.	Let's go to a sushi shop.
お寿司屋へ行きましょう。	

The particle **o** in Sentence Pattern 14 is the same **o** that was used in Lesson 2—**Biiru o kudasai**. That is, it shows the object of the verb—what you would like to do, eat, drink, etc. Compare the following:

Sukiyaki ga tabetai desu.	**Sukiyaki o tabemashō.**
すき焼きが食べたいです。	
Kimono ga kaitai desu.	**Kimono o kaimashō.**
着物が買いたいです。	
O-sake ga nomitai desu.	**O-sake o nomimashō.**
お酒が飲みたいです。	

Shimashō comes from the verb **suru** (this verb form will be explained later), which generally means "to do." It is the most frequently used Japanese verb because of its ability to allow an object-noun to function somewhat like a verb, much as "I do writing" might be equivalent to "I write" in English. Because many of the object-nouns used with **suru** were originally Chinese words, **suru** is often called the "Chinese verb". But since **suru** has now come to be used with many English and other foreign-language nouns as well, perhaps a better name for it would be the "foreign verb". The following are examples of nouns from English that are used with **suru** to express action.

Gorufu o shimashō.	Let's play golf.
ゴルフをしましょう。	
Tenisu o shimashō.	Let's play tennis.
テニスをしましょう。	
Dansu o shimashō.	Let's dance.
ダンスをしましょう。	
Bōringu o shimashō.	Let's bowl.
ボーリングをしましょう。	
Sukii o shimashō.	Let's ski.
スキーをしましょう。	

Practice

Practice repeating the following statements, replacing the object of the sentence each time.

1. At a restaurant:

Sukiyaki o tabemashō.	Let's eat sukiyaki.
すき焼きを食べましょう。	
Tenpura	tenpura.
てんぷら	
O-sushi	sushi.
お寿司	
Tonkatsu	pork cutlets.
とんかつ	
Biifusutēki	beefsteak.
ビーフステーキ	

2. At a coffee shop:

Kōhii o nomimashō.	Let's have (drink) coffee.
コーヒーを飲みましょう。	
Kōcha	black tea.
紅茶	
Kēki o tabemashō.	Let's have (eat) cake.
ケーキを食べましょう。	
Aisukuriimu	ice cream.
アイスクリーム	

3. At a bar:

Biiru o nomimashō.	Let's have (drink) beer.
ビールを飲みましょう。	
O-sake	sake.
お酒	

4. At a department store:

Kamera o kaimashō.　　　　　Let's buy a camera.
カメラを買いましょう。

Kono kamera　　　　　　　　this camera.
このカメラ

Sono rajio　　　　　　　　that radio (by you).
そのラジオ

5. On dates or other social occasions:

Gorufu o shimashō　　　　Let's play golf.
ゴルフをしましょう。

Tenisu　　　　　　　　　play tennis.
テニス

Bōringu　　　　　　　　go bowling.
ボーリング

Dansu　　　　　　　　　dance.
ダンス

Ano eiga o mimashō.　　　Let's see that movie.
あの映画を見ましょう。

Ano Kabuki　　　　　　that Kabuki play.
あの歌舞伎

Ano Bunraku　　　　　that puppet play.
あの文楽

Kono eiga　　　　　　this movie.
この映画

Nara e ikimashō.　　　　Let's go to Nara.
奈良へ行きましょう。

Ōsaka　　　　　　　　Osaka.
大阪

Kyōto　　　　　　　　Kyoto.
京都

Hiroshima　　　　　　Hiroshima.
広島

Asking for Suggestions

In this lesson you will learn a less abrupt way to suggest an activity to a friend or acquaintance by posing the suggestion as a question (Shall we …?). No new vocabulary is introduced.

Sentence Pattern 14A

NOUN + o / + VERB-INFINITIVE + -mashō ka? NOUN + を VERB-INFINITIVE + ましょうか？	Shall we + VERB + NOUN?

Examples

Sukiyaki o tabemashō ka?
すき焼きを食べましょうか？

Shall we eat sukiyaki?

Biiru o nomimashō ka?
ビールを飲みましょうか？

Shall we drink beer?

Kabuki o mimashō ka?
歌舞伎を見ましょうか？

Shall we see a Kabuki play?

Kimono o kaimashō ka?
着物を買いましょうか？

Shall we buy a kimono?

Tenisu o shimashō ka?
テニスをしましょうか？

Shall we play tennis?

Sentence Pattern 15A

PLACE [or] NOUN + e / ikimashō ka? PLACE [or] NOUN + へ行きましょうか？	Shall we go to + PLACE [or] NOUN.

Examples

Nihon e ikimashō ka?
日本へ行きましょうか？

Shall we go to Japan?

Eiga e ikimashō ka?
映画へ行きましょうか？

Shall we go to a movie?

Compare **Biiru o nomimashō** and **Biiru o nomimashō ka?** In both cases you are making a suggestion to someone else, but the question form is less abrupt because it asks directly for the other person's agreement. Since this latter type of suggestion is expressed as a question, one would usually answer in the following way:

Ē, tabemashō.　　　　　　　Yes, let's eat (it, some).
ええ。食べましょう。
Ē, nomimashō.　　　　　　　Yes, let's drink (it, some).
ええ。飲みましょう。

The following sentence patterns are very useful when you want to go somewhere or do something but don't know what to suggest.

Sentence Pattern 14B

Nani o / + VERB-INFINITIVE + **-mashō ka?** 何を + VERB-INFINITIVE + ましょうか？	What shall we + VERB?
Dore o / + VERB-INFINITIVE + **-mashō ka?** どれを + VERB-INFINITIVE + ましょうか？	Which one shall we + VERB?

Examples

Nani o (Dore o) tabemashō ka?　　What (Which one) shall we eat?
何を（どれを）食べましょうか？
Nani o (Dore o) nomimashō ka?　　What (Which one) shall we drink?
何を（どれを）飲みましょうか？
Nani o (Dore o) shimashō ka?　　What (Which one) shall we do?
何を（どれを）しましょうか？

Sentence Pattern 15B

Doko e / ikimashō ka? どこへ行きましょうか？	Where shall we go?

Practice

1. Practice saying the following short dialogues aloud.

Nani o tabemashō ka? 何を食べましょうか？	What shall we eat?
Biifusutēki o tabemashō. ビーフステーキを食べましょう。	Let's have steak.
Nani o nomimashō ka? 何を飲みましょうか？	What shall we drink?
O-sake o nomimashō. お酒を飲みましょう。	Let's drink sake.
Nani o shimashō ka? 何をしましょうか？	What shall we do?
Tenisu o shimashō. テニスをしましょう。	Let's play tennis.
Doko e ikimashō ka? どこへ行きましょうか？	Where shall we go?
Kyōto e ikimashō. 京都へ行きましょう。	Let's go to Kyoto.
Nani o kaimashō ka? 何を買いましょうか？	What shall we buy?
Kamera o kaimashō. カメラを買いましょう。	Let's buy a camera.
Nani o mimashō ka? 何を見ましょうか？	What shall we see?
Ano eiga o mimashō. あの映画を見ましょう。	Let's see that movie.

2. Translate the following into Japanese. Turn to pages 236–237 for answers.

   (a) Let's bowl.
   (b) Let's study.
   (c) Let's go to Kyoto.
   (d) Let's take a walk.

(e) Let's play tennis.

(f) Let's play golf.

(g) Let's practice.

(h) Let's go to Mt Fuji.

(i) Let's eat **sukiyaki**.

(j) Let's buy this camera,

(k) Let's go to that movie.

(l) Let's drink sake.

(m) Let's go to that photo studio.

(n) Let's go to the train station.

(o) Let's see this **Kabuki** play.

(p) Let's drink tea.

3. Practice repeating these short dialogues aloud.

Dore o kaimashō ka? どれを買いましょうか？	Which one shall we buy?
Kono kamera o kaimashō ka? このカメラを買いましょうか？	Shall we buy this camera?
Ē, kaimashō. ええ、買いましょう。	Yes, let's buy it.
Doko e ikimashō ka? どこへ行きましょうか？	Where shall we go?
Kyōto e ikimashō ka? 京都へ行きましょうか？	Shall we go to Kyoto?
Kyōto e ikitai desu ka? 京都へ行きたいですか？	Would you like to go to Kyoto?
Hai, ikitai desu. はい、行きたいです。	Yes, I'd like to.
Ano eiga ga mitai desu ka? あの映画が見たいですか？	Would you like to see that movie?
Iie. Mitaku arimasen. いいえ、見たくありません。	No, I wouldn't.
Doko e ikimashō ka? どこへ行きましょうか？	Where shall we go?

Kabuki e ikimashō ka?
歌舞伎へ行きましょうか？

Shall we go to Kabuki?

Ē, ikimashō.
ええ、行きましょう。

Yes, let's go.

Are wa nan desu ka?
あれは何ですか？

What's that?

Are wa jinja desu. Mitai desu ka?
あれは神社です。見たいですか？

That's a shrine. Would you like to see it?

Hai. Mitai desu. Ikimashō ka?
はい、みたいです。行きましょうか？

Yes, I would. Shall we go?

Ē, ikimashō.
ええ。行きましょう。

Yes, let's go.

Kore wa nan desu ka?
これは何ですか？

What is this?

Sore wa unagi desu. Tabetai desu ka?
それはうなぎです。食べたいですか？

That's eel. Would you like to eat some?

Iie, tabetaku arimasen.
いいえ、食べたくありません。

No, I wouldn't.

Nani ga tabetai desu ka?
何が食べたいですか？

What would you like to eat?

Kore to kore wa nan desu ka?
これとこれは何ですか？

What are these things here?

Sore wa teishoku desu. Tabemashō ka?
それは定食です。食べましょうか？

That's the full-course dinner. Shall we eat that?

Ē, tabemashō.
ええ。食べましょう。

Yes, let's eat that.

OTHER USEFUL VERBS

Some useful new verbs and examples of the particles used with them are listed below in sentence form. Dropping the -mashō at the end of each verb will give you the verb-infinitive, to which you can add the -tai desu ending that you have already studied or other verb endings that will be presented later. Alternative particles are given in parentheses.

NOUN + o agemashō. NOUN + をあげましょう。	Let's give + NOUN.
NOUN + o araimashō. NOUN + を洗いましょう。	Let's wash + NOUN.
NOUN + o dashimashō. NOUN + を出しましょう。	Let's mail + NOUN.
NOUN + o hajimemashō. NOUN + を始めましょう。	Let's begin + NOUN.
NOUN + o kaeshimashō. NOUN + を返しましょう。	Let's return + NOUN.
NOUN + o kakimashō. NOUN + を書きましょう。	Let's write + NOUN.
NOUN + o karimashō. NOUN + を借りましょう。	Let's borrow + NOUN.
NOUN + o kashimashō. NOUN + を貸しましょう。	Let's lend + NOUN.
NOUN + o naraimashō. NOUN + を習いましょう。	Let's learn + NOUN.
NOUN + o okurimashō. NOUN + を送りましょう。	Let's send + NOUN.
NOUN + o tsukurimashō. NOUN + を作りましょう。	Let's make + NOUN.
NOUN + o yamemashō. NOUN + をやめましょう。	Let's stop + NOUN.
NOUN + o yomimashō. NOUN + を読みましょう。	Let's read + NOUN.
PERSON + ni (to) aimashō. PERSON + に（と）会いましょう。	Let's meet + SOMEONE.

PERSON + **o machimashō.**
PERSON + を待ちましょう。

Let's wait for + PERSON.

PERSON + **o yobimashō.**
PERSON + を呼びましょう。

Let's call + PERSON.

PLACE + **de machimashō.**
PLACE + で待ちましょう。

Let's wait at + PLACE.

PLACE + **de orimashō.**
PLACE + で降りましょう。

Let's get off at + PLACE.

PLACE + **e (ni) hairimashō.**
PLACE + へ（に）入りましょう。

Let's enter + PLACE.

PLACE + **ni suwarimashō.**
PLACE + に座りましょう。

Let's sit at + PLACE.

VEHICLE + **ni norimashō.**
VEHICLE + に乗りましょう。

Let's get in (on) + VEHICLE.

VEHICLE + **kara (o) orimashō.**
VEHICLE + から（を）降りましょう。

Let's get off + VEHICLE.

Arukimashō.
歩きましょう。

Let's walk.

Dekakemashō.
出かけましょう。

Let's go out.

Demashō.
出ましょう。

Let's leave (this place).

Denwa o kakemashō.
電話をかけましょう。

Let's make a telephone call.

Gakko o yasumimashō.
学校を休みましょう。

Let's not go to class.

Hanashimashō.
話しましょう。

Let's talk.

Hidari e (ni) magarimashō.
左へ（に）曲がりましょう。

Let's turn to the left.

Iimashō.
言いましょう。

Let's say (this).

Isogimashō.
急ぎましょう。

Let's hurry.

Kaerimashō.
帰りましょう。

Let's return home.

Kaisha o yasumimashō.
会社を休みましょう。

Let's not go to work.

Kangaemashō.
考えましょう。

Let's think (about that).

Kikimashō.
聞きましょう。

Let's listen (or inquire).

Kimemashō.
決めましょう。

Let's decide on this.

Koko o magarimashō.
ここを曲がりましょう。

Let's turn here.

Migi e (ni) magarimashō.
右へ (に) 曲がりましょう。

Let's turn to the right.

Nemashō.
寝ましょう。

Let's go to sleep.

Norikaemashō.
乗り換えましょう。

Let's transfer (trains).

O-kane o haraimashō.
お金を払いましょう。

Let's pay the money.

Yasumimashō.
休みましょう。

Let's rest.

Chapter 5
(Lessons 17 – 21)

Sentence Patterns Covered in Chapter 5	
Sentence Pattern 16	ADJECTIVE + **desu.** ADJECTIVE + です。
Sentence Pattern 16A	TOPIC + **wa /** + ADJECTIVE + **desu.** TOPIC + は + ADJECTIVE + です。
Sentence Pattern 17	ADJECTIVE + NOUN + **desu.** ADJECTIVE + NOUN です。
Sentence Pattern 17A	TOPIC + **wa /** + ADJECTIVE + NOUN + **desu.** TOPIC + は + ADJECTIVE + NOUN です。
Sentence Pattern 18	ADJECTIVAL NOMINATIVE + **desu.** ADJECTIVAL NOMINATIVE + です。 TOPIC + **wa /** + ADJECTIVE NOMINATIVE + **desu.** TOPIC + は + ADJECTIVE NOMINATIVE + です。
Sentence Pattern 18A	TOPIC (PERSON) + **wa /** + NOUN + **ga / suki desu.** TOPIC (PERSON) + は + NOUN + が好きです。 TOPIC (PERSON) + **wa /** + NOUN + **ga / kirai desu.** TOPIC (PERSON) + は + NOUN + が嫌いです。 TOPIC (PERSON) + **wa /** + NOUN + **ga / jōzu desu.** TOPIC (PERSON) + は + NOUN + が上手です。 TOPIC (PERSON) + **wa /** + NOUN + **ga / heta desu.** TOPIC (PERSON) + は + NOUN + が下手です。

Sentence Pattern 18B	TOPIC (PERSON) + wa / nani ga / suki desu ka?
	TOPIC (PERSON) + は何が好きですか？
	TOPIC (PERSON) + wa / nani ga / kirai desuka?
	TOPIC (PERSON) + は何が嫌いですか？
	TOPIC (PERSON) + wa / nani ga / jōzu desuka?
	TOPIC (PERSON) + は何が上手ですか？
	TOPIC (PERSON) + wa / nani ga / heta desuka?
	TOPIC (PERSON) + は何が下手ですか？
Sentence Pattern 19	ADJECTIVE NOMINATIVE + na+ NOUN + desu.
	ADJECTIVE NOMINATIVE + な+ NOUN + です。
	TOPIC + wa / + ADJECTIVE NOMINATIVE + na+ NOUN + desu.
	TOPIC + は + ADJECTIVE NOMINATIVE + な + NOUN + です。

If you are brought to restaurants or scenic places in Japan, you will want to be able to show your appreciation to your host by commenting on how good the food is or how beautiful the view. If you are traveling around Japan by yourself, you will want to be able to tell the innkeeper or the waiter what your preferences are. The adjectives and descriptive nouns presented in this chapter will help you to do just that.

Dialogue

勇輝 ： それは何ですか？
春樹 ： これはアンパンマンのアニメです。
勇輝 ： 新しいアニメですか？
春樹 ： いいえ、新しくありません。とても古いです。
勇輝 ： 古いアニメが好きですか？
春樹 ： 時々好きです。でも嫌いな物もあります。
勇輝 ： アンパンマンは小さいですね。
春樹 ： そうですね。
勇輝 ： アンパンマンは何が上手ですか？
春樹 ： アンパンマンは強いです。
勇輝 ： あれは何ですか？
春樹 ： あれは梅干しです。
勇輝 ： 甘いですか？すっぱいですか？
春樹 ： とてもすっぱいです。
勇輝 ： 高かったですか？
春樹 ： いいえ、安かったです。
勇輝 ： 良かったですね！

Yūki	: **Sore wa nan desu ka?**	What is that (by you, that you are watching)?
Haruki	: **Kore wa Anpanman no anime desu.**	This is an anime about Anpanman.
Yūki	: **Atarashii anime desu ka?**	Is it a new anime?
Haruki	: **Iie, atarashiku arimasen. Totemo furui desu.**	No, it isn't new. It's very old.
Yūki	: **Furui anime ga suki desu ka?**	Do you like old anime?

Haruki	:	Tokidoki suki desu. Demo kirai na mono mo arimasu.	I like them sometimes. But there are also some I don't like.
Yūki	:	Anpanman wa chiisai desu ne.	Anpanman is small, isn't he?
Haruki	:	Sō desu ne.	That's right.
Yūki	:	Anpanman wa nani ga jōzu desuka?	What is Anpanman good at?
Haruki	:	Anpanman wa tsuyoi desu.	Anpanman is strong.
Yūki	:	Are wa nan desu ka?	What is that (over there)?
Haruki	:	Are wa umeboshi desu.	That is **umeboshi**.
Yūki	:	Amai desuka? Suppai desuka?	Is it sweet or sour?
Haruki	:	Totemo suppai desu.	It's really sour.
Yūki	:	Takakatta desu ka?	Was it expensive?
Haruki	:	Iie, yasukatta desu.	No, it was cheap.
Yūki	:	Yokatta desu ne!	That was good, wasn't it!

Dialogue vocabulary

amai	甘い	sweet
anime	アニメ	cartoon film
atarashii	新しい	new
atarashiku arimasen	新しくありません	not new
furui	古い	old
jōzu	上手	(be) good at; skillful
kirai	嫌いな	hate/don't like
mo	も	also
suki	好き	like
takakatta	高かった	was expensive
tsuyoi	強い	strong
totemo	とても	very
umeboshi	梅干し	pickled plum
wakatta	若かった	was young
yasakatta	安かった	was cheap
yokatta	よかった	was good

Describing Things

In this lesson you will learn many Japanese adjectives that can be used to describe persons, places, or things. You will also learn how to conjugate these adjectives and how to use them in a sentence. Also, several terms used to describe time are introduced.

Vocabulary

Adjectives

atarashii	新しい	new; fresh
furui	古い	old; used (for things)
hayai	早い	fast; early
osoi	遅い	slow; late
hiroi	広い	spacious; wide
semai	狭い	cramped; narrow
ii	いい	good
warui	悪い	bad
katai	かたい	hard, tough (texture)
yawarakai	やわらかい	soft, tender (texture)
nagai	長い	long
mijikai	短い	short
ōi	多い	plentiful; large in portion
sukunai	少ない	scarce; skimpy in portion
ōkii	大きい	big, large
chiisai	小さい	small
takai	高い	expensive; high
hikui	低い	low
yasui	安い	inexpensive, cheap
tōi	遠い	far
chikai	近い	near
wakai	若い	young
atatakai (attakai)	暖かい/温かい （あったかい）	warm (weather, objects, persons)

suzushii	涼しい	cool (weather)
mushiatsui	蒸し暑い	muggy, hot and humid
atsui	暑い/熱い	hot (weather, objects)
samui	寒い	cold (weather)
tsumetai	冷たい	cold (to the touch)
amai	甘い	sweet tasting
karai	辛い	salty; soy-saucy; spicy
nigai	苦い	bitter
suppai	すっぱい	sour
oishii	おいしい	tasty; delicious
mazui	まずい	not tasty; unappetizing
omoshiroi	おもしろい	interesting; entertaining; funny
tanoshii	楽しい	enjoyable
tsumaranai	つまらない	uninteresting; boring; not enjoyable
yasashii	やさしい	easy, simple; tender (person)
muzukashii	難しい	difficult; fussy (person)
isogashii	忙しい	busy
kanashii	悲しい	sad
sabishii	淋しい	lonely
ureshii	嬉しい	glad
uttōshii	うっとおしい	depressing; oppressive

Nouns

densha	電車	electric train
Eigo	英語	the English language
hi	日	day
hito	人	person
Nihongo	日本語	the Japanese language
o-ryōri	お料理	cooking; cuisine
o-tenki	お天気	the weather
piano	ピアノ	piano
shinkansen	新幹線	high-speed bullet train
uchi (ie)	家	home (house)

Adverbs of Time

ashita	明日	tomorrow
kinō	昨日	yesterday
kyō	今日	today
kesa	今朝	this morning
konban	今晩	this evening
konogoro	この頃	these days

Culture and vocabulary notes

In English, "old" is used to describe both people and things. In Japanese, however, the adjective **furui** applies only to things. Although **wakai** is used to describe an individual who is young, there is no Japanese adjective meaning "old" to characterize people. Instead, Japanese people use the noun **toshiyori** to designate an elderly person.

The word "cold" is used in English to describe both weather and the temperature of objects. In Japanese, **samui** is used for cold weather, and **tsumetai** is used for objects cold to the touch. **Atsui** is used to describe hot weather or an object that is hot to the touch. However, **atsui** is not used with the word for "water." Instead, the noun **o-yu** is used for hot or boiling water.

Yasashii, which can mean "tender" when referring to the character of a person, never refers to food in Japanese. For tender meat or items having a soft texture, **yawarakai** is used. Hardness or toughness is expressed by **katai**.

The word **uchi** is often used to mean "household" or "family." It can also be used like the word "house" in English, but normally **ie** is used to designate "house."

Grammar

Sentence Pattern 16	
ADJECTIVE + **desu.** ADJECTIVE + です。	It is + ADJECTIVE.

Examples

Atarashii desu. 新しいです。	It's new.
Nagai desu. 長いです。	It's long.

Takai desu.　　　　　　　　　It's expensive.
高いです。

Atsui desu.　　　　　　　　　It's hot.
暑いです。

Oishii desu.　　　　　　　　It's delicious.
おいしいです。

Omoshiroi desu.　　　　　　It's interesting.
おもしろいです。

Muzukashii desu.　　　　　It's difficult.
難しいです。

Remember that **desu** was used in Chapter 2 to make the sentence **Tabetai desu** more polite. Similarly, to say **Takai** rather than **Takai desu** means the same thing but is considered informal.

As noted in Chapter 4, you will often hear Japanese use the exclamatory word **ne** at the end of a sentence or phrase, particularly when that sentence or phrase contains an adjective. For example, the **ne** in **Takai desu ne** invites the listener to agree with the speaker. Often the pronunciation is prolonged to **nē** for emphasis.

Practice
Practice saying the following sentences aloud

Takai desu ne.　　　　It's expensive, isn't it?
高いですね。

Yasui desu ne.　　　　It's cheap, isn't it?
安いですね。

Ōkii desu ne.　　　　It's big, isn't it?
大きいですね。

Chiisai desu ne.　　　It's small, isn't it?
小さいですね。

Nagai desu ne.　　　It's long, isn't it?
長いですね。

Mijikai desu ne.　　It's short, isn't it?
短いですね。

Ii desu ne.　　　　It's good, isn't it?
いいですね。

Warui desu ne. 悪いですね。	It's bad, isn't it?
Tōi desu ne. 遠いですね。	It's far, isn't it?
Chikai desu ne. 近いですね。	It's near, isn't it?
Hayai desu ne. 早いですね。	It's fast, isn't it? [or] It's early, isn't it?
Osoi desu ne. 遅いですね。	It's slow, isn't it? [or] It's late, isn't it?

THE CONJUGATION OF ADJECTIVES

Unlike English adjectives, Japanese adjectives take new forms to denote past and negative usages. As you may have already noticed, Japanese adjectives all end in -i. What precedes this -i is called the adjective stem, to which past and negative endings are added.

The Polite Past Affirmative

You form the polite past tense of adjectives by adding -**katta** *desu* to the adjective stem.

Examples

	adjective stem	polite present	polite past
1)	ōki- 大き-	Ōkii desu. 大きいです。 It is big.	Ōkikatta desu. 大きかったです。 It was big.
2)	oso- 遅-	Osoi desu. 遅いです。 It is slow. [or] It is late.	Osokatta desu. 遅かったです。 It was slow. [or] It was late.

The **desu** here only serves to make the adjective polite. **Ōkikatta** by itself is past tense and informal.

The Polite Present Negative

You form the polite negative of adjectives by adding -**ku arimasen** to the adjective stem.

Examples

	adjective stem	polite present	polite pres./neg
1)	ōki- 大き-	Ōkii desu. 大きいです。 It is big.	Ōkiku arimasen. 大きくありません。 It is not big.

2) oso- 遅−	Osoi desu. 遅いです。 It is slow. [or] It is late.	Osoku arimasen. 遅くありません。 It is not slow. [or] It is not late.	

The Polite Past Negative

You form the polite past negative of adjectives by adding **deshita** to the polite present negative.

Examples

	adjective stem	polite present	polite pres./neg	polite past/neg.
1)	ōki- 大きき−	Ōkii desu. 大きいです。 It is big.	Ōkikku arimasen. 大きくありま せん。 It is not big.	Ōkiku arimasen deshita. 大きくありま せんでした。 It was not big.
2)	oso- 遅−	Osoi desu. 遅いです。 It is slow. [or] It is late.	Osoku arimasen. 遅くありま せん。 It is not slow. [or] It is not late.	Osoku arimasen deshita. 遅くありませ んでした。 It was not slow. [or] It was not late.

Deshita (as in **Ōkiku arimasen deshita***)* is the past tense of **desu. Ii**, "good," is the only adjective whose stem is irregular. The adjective stem of **ii** is **yo-**, based on **yoi**, an older form of **ii**.

polite present	Ii desu. いいです。	It is good.
adjective stem	yo- 良−	(adjective stem)
polite past	Yokatta desu. 良かったです。	It was good.
polite pres./neg.	Yoku arimasen. 良くありません。	It is not good.
polite past/neg.	Yoku arimasen deshita. 良くありませんでした。	It was not good.

SUMMARY OF ADJECTIVE CONJUGATION
(POLITE FORMS)

Adj. (informal)	Meaning	Adjective Stem	Present	Past	Present Negative	Past Negative
ōkii 大きい	big	ōki- 大きー	Ōkii desu. 大きいです。	Ōkikatta desu. 大きかったです。	Ōkiku arimasen. 大きくありません。	Ōkiku arimasen deshita. 大きくありませんでした。
atarashii 新しい	new	atarashi- 新しー	Atarashii desu. 新しいです。	Atarashikatta desu. 新しかったです。	Atarashiku arimasen. 新しくありません。	Atarashiku arimasen deshita. 新しくありませんでした。
hayai 早い	fast; early	haya- 早ー	Hayai desu. 早いです。	Hayakatta desu. 早かったです。	Hayaku arimasen. 早くありません。	Hayaku arimasen deshita. 早くありませんでした。
ii いい	good	yo- 良	Ii desu. いいです。	Yokatta desu. 良かったです。	Yoku arimasen. 良くありません。	Yoku arimasen deshita. 良くありませんでした。
warui 悪い	bad	waru- 悪ー	Warui desu. 悪いです。	Warukatta desu. 悪かったです。	Waruku arimasen. 悪くありません。	Waruku arimasen deshita. 悪くありませんでした。
oishii おいしい	delicious	oishi- おいしー	Oishii desu. おいしいです。	Oishikatta desu. おいしかったです。	Oishiku arimasen. おいしくありません。	Oishiku arimasen deshita. おいしくありませんでした。
takai 高い	expensive	taka- 高ー	Takai desu. 高いです。	Takakatta desu. 高かったです。	Takaku arimasen. 高くありません。	Takaku arimasen deshita. 高くありませんでした。
yasui 安い	cheap	yasu- 安ー	Yasui desu. 安いです。	Yasukatta desu. 安かったです。	Yasuku arimasen. 安くありません。	Yasuku arimasen deshita. 安くありませんでした。
omoshiroi おもしろい	interesting	omoshiro- おもしろー	Omoshiroi desu. おもしろいです。	Omoshirokatta desu. おもしろかったです。	Omoshiroku arimasen. おもしろくありません。	Omoshiroku arimasen deshita. おもしろくありませんでした。

Practice

1. Translate the following sentences into Japanese. Turn to page 237 to see the answers.

  (a) It's expensive, isn't it?

  (b) It's cheap, isn't it?

  (c) It's large, isn't it?

  (d) It's small, isn't it?

  (e) It's long, isn't it?

  (f) It's short, isn't it?

2. Form the polite present negative for each sentence as shown in the example below.

  Example: Takai desu. → Takaku arimasen.

  Yasui desu.
  安いです。

  Suzushii desu.
  涼しいです。

  Hiroi desu.
  広いです。

  Atatakai desu.
  暖かい（温かい）です。

  Semai desu.
  狭いです。

  Nagai desu.
  長いです。

  Atsui desu.
  暑い（熱い）です。

  Mijikai desu.
  短いです。

  Samui desu.
  寒いです。

3. Form the polite past for each sentence as shown in the example below.

  Example: Karai desu. → Karakatta desu.

  Amai desu.
  甘いです。

  Chiisai desu.
  小さいです。

  Atarashii desu.
  新しいです。

  Ōkii desu.
  大きいです。

  Furui desu.
  古いです。

  Ii desu.
  いいです。

  Wakai desu.
  若いです。

  Warui desu.
  悪いです。

4. Form the polite past negative for each sentence as shown in the example below.

Example: Tōi desu. → Tōku arimasen deshita.

Chikai desu.	**Oishii desu.**
近いです。	おいしいです。
Omoshiroi desu.	**Mazui desu.**
おもしろいです。	まずいです。
Tsumaranai desu.	**Yasashii desu.**
つまらないです。	やさしいです。
Atsui desu.	**Muzukashii desu.**
暑い (熱い) です。	難しいです。
Samui desu.	
寒いです。	

Describing Things (continued)

In this lesson you will learn different ways to use adjectives, including how to combine adjectives and nouns. There is no new vocabulary introduced in this lesson.

Grammar

Sentence Pattern 16A	
TOPIC + **wa** / + ADJECTIVE + **desu.** TOPIC + は + ADJECTIVE + です。	TOPIC + is + ADJECTIVE.

Examples

Kore wa takai desu.
これは高いです。

This is expensive.

Are wa oishii desu.
あれはおいしいです。

That is delicious.

Sore wa atarashii desu.
それは新しいです。

It is new.

Kono kamera wa takai desu.
このカメラは高いです。

This camera is expensive.

Kono sūpu wa oishii desu.
このスープはおいしいです。

This soup is delicious.

Remember that **wa** denotes the topic of the sentence—what you are talking or asking about. The above sentence pattern can also be used with the past tense of adjectives and with the present and past negative forms.

Kono kamera wa takakatta desu.
このカメラは高かったです。

This camera was expensive.

Ano sūpu wa oishiku arimasen.
あのスープはおいしくありません。

That soup does not taste good.

Sono terebi wa yoku arimasen deshita.
そのテレビは良くありませんでした。

That television set was not good.

Now compare the following sentence pattern with Sentence Pattern 16A.

Sentence Pattern 17	
ADJECTIVE + NOUN + **desu.**	It's a + ADJECTIVE + NOUN.
ADJECTIVE + NOUN + です。	

Examples

Takai terebi desu.
高いテレビです。
It's an expensive television set.

Yasui rajio desu.
安いラジオです。
It's an inexpensive radio.

Atarashii terebi desu.
新しいテレビです。
It's a new television set.

Furui terebi desu.
古いテレビです。
It's an old television set.

Ii kamera desu.
いいカメラです。
It's a good camera.

Warui kamera desu.
悪いカメラです。
It's a poor camera.

Omoshiroi eiga desu.
おもしろい映画です。
It's an interesting movie.

Tanoshii eiga desu.
楽しい映画です。
It's an enjoyable movie.

Tsumaranai eiga desu.
つまらい映画です。
It's a boring movie.

Now compare Sentence Patterns 16A and 17 in the polite past tense.

S.P. 16A: Eiga wa omoshirokatta desu.
映画はおもしろかったです。
The movie was interesting.

S.P. 17: Omoshiroi eiga deshita.
おもしろい映画でした。
It was an interesting movie.

Compare Sentence Patterns 16A and 17 in the polite present negative form.

S.P. 16A: Eiga wa omoshiroku arimasen.　　The movie is not interesting.
映画はおもしろくありません。

S.P. 17:　Omoshiroi eiga ja arimasen.　　It is not an interesting movie.
おもしろい映画じゃありま
せん。

Compare Sentence Patterns 16A and 17 in the polite past negative form.

S.P. 16A: Eiga wa omoshiroku arimasen　　The movie was not interesting.
　　deshita.
映画はおもしろくありませんでした。

S.P. 17:　Omoshiroi eiga ja arimasen　　It was not an interesting movie.
　　deshita.
おもしろい映画じゃありませんでした。

The addition of a topic to Sentence Pattern 17 results in the following kind of sentence.

Sentence Pattern 17A	
TOPIC + **wa** / + ADJECTIVE + NOUN + **desu.**	TOPIC is a + ADJECTIVE +
TOPIC + は + ADJECTIVE + NOUN + です。	NOUN .

Examples

Kore wa oishii tenpura desu.　　This is a delicious plate of **tenpura**.
これはおいしい天ぷらです。

Are wa takai resutoran desu.　　That is an expensive restaurant.
あれは高いレストランです。

Tanaka-san wa ii sensei desu.　　Mr. Tanaka is a good teacher.
田中さんはいい先生です。

Study carefully the following examples of the patterns you have learned so far in this chapter. Note their similarities and differences.

S.P. 16:　Atarashii desu.
新しいです。

S.P. 16A: Kono terebi wa / atarashii desu.
このテレビは新しいです。

S.P. 17:   Atarashii terebi desu.
新しいテレビです。

S.P. 17A: Kore wa / atarashii terebi desu.
これは新しいテレビです。

Practice

1. Practice with Sentence Pattern 16A.

(a) Use any of the following topics and adjectives together to make reasonable sentences that contain polite present adjective forms.

Example: Kono terebi wa atarashii desu.
このテレビは新しいです。

Topics	Adjectives
eiga 映画	tsumaranai つまらない
terebi テレビ	atarashii 新しい
o-sushi お寿司	oishii おいしい
yūbinkyoku 郵便局	takai 高い
Nihon 日本	tōi 遠い
kamera カメラ	semai 狭い
kore, sore, are これ、それ、あれ	omoshiroi おもしろい
kono, sono, ano + NOUN この、その、あの + NOUN	nagai 長い
	chiisai 小さい
	yasui 安い

(b) Now use the word list in (a) to make sentences containing polite past, polite present negative, and polite past negative adjective forms.

Examples:

Sono terebi wa atarashikatta desu.	Sono terebi wa atarashiku arimasen.	Sono terebi wa atarashiku arimasen deshita.
そのテレビは新しかったです。	そのテレビは新しくありません。	そのテレビは新しくありませんでした。

2. Practice with Sentence Pattern 17.
   (a) Point to things in your room and describe them.

   Example: Takai kamera desu.
   高いカメラです。

   (b) Think of some things you used to own and describe them.

   Example: Takai kamera deshita.
   高いカメラでした。

3. Practice with Sentence Pattern 17A.
   (a) Point to things in your room and describe them.

   Examples:

Kore wa atarashii terebi desu.	Are wa ii kamera desu.
これはあたらしいテレビです。	あれはいいカメラです。

   (b) Now describe things as they were in the past.

   Examples:

Kore wa atarashii terebi deshita.	Sore wa ii kamera deshita.
これはあたらしいテレビでした。	それはいいカメラでした。

(c) Recall several movies you have seen and describe them. Use adjectives like **ii**, **warui**, **tsumaranai**, **tanoshii**, **atarashii**, and **furui**.

Examples:

NAME OF THE MOVIE
  wa omoshiroi eiga deshita.
NAME OF THE MOVIE はおも
  しろい映画でした。

Ano eiga wa omoshiroi eiga ja arimasen deshita.
あの映画はおもしろい映画じゃ
  ありませんでした。

(d) Recall a meal you have eaten and describe it.

Examples:

Are wa oishii tenpura deshita.
あれはおいしい天ぷらでした。
Are wa mazui tenpura deshita.
あれはまずい天ぷらでした。
Are wa takai hanbāgā deshita.
あれは高いハンバーガーでした。

Talking about This and That

In this lesson you will mainly review a large number of adjectives and adjectival phrases and the situations in which they are commonly used. A few new vocabulary terms are introduced.

1. TALKING ABOUT THE WEATHER

Vocabulary

The following list of words and phrases will come in handy when talking to a friend about the weather. You will find that Japanese frequently comment on the weather, often as part of a greeting to someone.

atatakai (attakai)	暖かい/温かい （あったかい）	warm
suzushii	涼しい	cool
atsui	暑い/熱い	hot
samui	寒い	cold
mushiatsui	蒸し暑い	muggy
ii o-tenki	いいお天気	good weather
warui o-tenki	悪いお天気	bad weather
uttōshii o-tenki	うっとうしいお天気	depressing (*or* oppressive) weather

Practice

Now practice Sentence Pattern 16A by saying the following sentences aloud.

Kyō wa samui desu ne. 今日は寒いですね。	It's cold today, isn't it?
Kyō wa atsui desu ne. 今日は暑いですね。	It's hot today, isn't it?
Kyō wa mushiatsui desu ne. 今日は蒸し暑いですね。	It's muggy today, isn't it?
Kinō wa samukatta desu ne. 今日は寒かったですね。	It was cold yesterday, wasn't it?

Kesa wa atsukatta desu ne.
今朝は暑かったですね。

It was hot this morning, wasn't it?

Konogoro wa atsui desu ne.
この頃は暑いですね。

It's hot these days, isn't it?

Now practice Sentence Pattern 17A by saying the following sentences aloud.

Kyō wa ii o-tenki desu ne.
今日はいいお天気ですね。

It's good weather today, isn't it?

Konogoro wa uttōshii o-tenki desu ne.
この頃はうっとうしいお天気で
すね。

It's depressing weather these days,
isn't it?

2. TALKING ABOUT FOOD

Vocabulary

The following list gives various adjectives that can be used to describe food.

oishii	おいしい	tasty; delicious
mazui	まずい	not tasty; unappetizing
takai	高い	expensive
yasui	安い	inexpensive, cheap
atarashii	新しい	new; fresh
furui	古い	old; stale
ii	いい	good
warui	悪い	bad
atsui	暑い/熱い	hot
tsumetai	冷たい	cold (to the taste or touch)
amai	甘い	sweet
karai	辛い	salty; soy-saucy; spicy
nigai	苦い	bitter
suppai	すっぱい	sour
ōi	多い	large in portion
sukunai	少ない	few, skimpy in portion

Practice

Practice using these adjectives to describe some common foods.

oishii tonkatsu
おいしいトンカツ
delicious pork cutlet

atarashii o-sashimi
新しいお刺身
fresh **sashimi**

takai o-sushi
高いお寿司
expensive sushi

yasui resutoran
安いレストラン
inexpensive restaurant

furui pan
古いパン
stale bread

ii biifusutēki
いいビーフステーキ
good steak

warui o-sashimi
悪いお刺身
bad **sashimi**

mazui tenpura
まずい天ぷら
bad-tasting **tenpura**

tsumetai sūpu
冷たいスープ
cold soup

amai kēki
甘いケーキ
sweet cake

atsui kōhii
熱いコーヒー
hot coffee

Now practice saying these sentences aloud.

Kore wa oishii tenpura desu ne.
これはおいしい天ぷらですね。
This is a delicious plate of **tenpura**, isn't it?

Kore wa takai resutoran desu ne.
これは高いレストランですね。
This is an expensive restaurant, isn't it?

Kore wa amai desu ne.
これは甘いですね。
This is sweet, isn't it?

Kore wa ōi desu ne.
これは多いですね。
This is a lot (This is a large portion), isn't it?

Kore wa sukunai desu ne.
これは少ないですね。
This is skimpy (This is a small portion), isn't it?

3. TALKING ABOUT PEOPLE

Vocabulary

The following list gives various adjectives that can be used to describe people.

ōkii hito	大きい人	a large person
chiisai hito	小さい人	a small person
ii hito	いい人	a good person
warui hito	悪い人	a bad person
yasashii hito	やさしい人	a tender-hearted person; a kind person
muzukashii hito	難しい人	a fussy person; a person who is particular
omoshiroi hito	おもしろい人	an interesting person; an amusing person
atatakai hito	温かい人	a warm person
isogashii hito	忙しい人	a busy person

Practice

Now practice saying these sentences aloud.

Tanaka-san wa ii hito desu. Mr. Tanaka is a good person.
田中さんはいい人です。

Yamada-san wa muzukashii hito desu. Mrs. Yamada is a fussy person.
山田さんは難しい人です。

Kazuko-san wa yasashii hito desu. Kazuko is a kind person.
和子さんはやさしい人です。

Tanaka-san wa isogashii hito desu. Mr. Tanaka is a busy person.
田中さんは忙しい人です。

4. TALKING ABOUT YOURSELF

Practice these sentences to help you describe your feelings or situation.

Ureshii desu. I'm happy. / I'm glad.
嬉しいです。

Kanashii desu. I'm sad.
悲しいです。

Isogashii desu. I'm busy.
忙しいです。

Sabishii desu. I'm lonely.
淋しいです。

Culture and vocabulary notes

The above words, and most other words that describe emotions or states of being, should usually only be used in reference to yourself or when asking about someone you are talking with. Japanese hesitate to state with certainty about the inner feelings that others may have.

5. TALKING ABOUT THINGS

Vocabulary

depāto	デパート	a department store
shinkansen	新幹線	a high-speed "bullet" train
yukata	浴衣	a simple cotton kimono, generally worn in summer

Practice

Practice these phrases that will help you comment on the things around you.

tōi daigaku　　　　　　a distant university
遠い大学

chikai yūbinkyoku　　a nearby post office
近い郵便局

hiroi uchi　　　　　　　a spacious house
広い家

semai uchi　　　　　　　a cramped house
狭い家

takai depāto　　　　　an expensive department store
高いデパート

yasui resutoran　　　an inexpensive restaurant
安いレストラン

nagai kimono　　　　　a long kimono
長い着物

mijikai yukata　　　　a short **yukata**
短い浴衣

hayai shinkansen　　a fast bullet train
早い新幹線

osoi densha　　　　　　a slow electric train
遅い電車

tanoshii eiga　　　　　an enjoyable movie
楽しい映画

tsumaranai eiga つまらない映画	a boring movie
yasashii Nihongo やさしい日本語	easy Japanese
muzukashii Eigo 難しい英語	difficult English

Practice giving affirmative and negative answers to these questions.

Sono sētā wa takai desu ka? そのセーターは高いですか？	Is that sweater expensive?
Hai, takai desu. はい、高いです。	Yes, it's expensive.
Iie, takaku arimasen. いいえ、高くありません。	No, it isn't expensive.

Kono resutoran wa ii desu ka? このレストランはいいですか？	Is this restaurant good?
Ē, ii desu. ええ、いいです。	Yes, it's good.
Iie, yoku arimasen. いいえ、良くありません。	No, it isn't good.

Anata wa isogashii desu ka? あなたは忙しいですか？	Are you busy?
Ē, isogashii desu. ええ、忙しいです。	Yes, I'm busy.
Iie, isogashiku arimasen. いいえ、忙しくありません。	No, I'm not busy.

Yūbinkyoku wa tōi desu ka? 郵便局は遠いですか？	Is the post office far?
Hai, tōi desu. はい、遠いです。	Yes, it's far.
Iie, tōku arimasen. いいえ、遠くありません。	No, it's not far.

Tōkyō Daigaku wa ōkii desu ka?
東京退学は大きいですか？

Is Tokyo University large?

Hai, ōkii desu.
はい、大きいです。

Yes, it's large.

Iie, ōkiku arimasen.
いいえ、大きくありません。

No, it isn't large.

Using Another Kind of Descriptive Word

In this lesson you will learn about adjectival nominatives, which are nouns that can act like adjectives. These words can be used to describe a variety of people, places, and things.

Vocabulary

dame	だめ	bad; unskillful
genki	元気	healthy
heta	下手	(be) poor at, not skillful
hima	暇	(has) free time
jōzu	上手	(be) good at, skillful, adept
kirai	嫌い	distasteful; dislike
kirei	きれい	pretty; clean
shinsetsu	親切	kind
shizuka	静か	quiet
suki	好き	likable; be liked
suteki	素敵	wonderful; great
taikutsu	退屈	boring
yūmei	有名	famous

Culture and vocabulary notes

The words above are representative of another kind of descriptive word in Japanese. It is called the adjectival nominative. As its name implies, it is a noun that can communicate what English considers to be an adjectival meaning: "pretty," "healthy," "famous," and so on. Because it is a noun, though, it does not conjugate, and you should be careful not to mistake an adjectival nominative ending in -*i* for an adjective of the type you have just studied in previous lessons.

Grammar

Sentence Pattern 18	
ADJECTIVE NOMINATIVE + **desu.** ADJECTIVE NOMINATIVE です。	It's a + ADJECTIVE.
TOPIC + **wa** / + ADJECTIVE NOMINATIVE + **desu.** TOPIC + は + ADJECTIVE NOMINATIVE + です。	TOPIC + is + ADJECTIVE

Kirei desu. きれいです。	It's pretty. [or] It's clean.
Suteki desu. 素敵です。	It's wonderful.
Yūmei desu. 有名です。	It's famous.
Taikutsu desu. 退屈です。	It's boring. [or] I'm bored.
Shizuka desu. 静かです。	It's quiet.
Suki desu. 好きです。	I like (it).
Kirai desu. 嫌いです。	I dislike (it).
Dame desu. だめです。	It's no good.
Jōzu desu. 上手です。	(Someone) is good at (it).
Heta desu. 下手です。	(Someone) is poor at (it).
Tanaka-san wa genki desu. 田中さんは元気です。	Mr. Tanaka is healthy.
Yamada Sensei wa hima desu. 山田先生は暇です。	Professor Yamada has lots of free time.
O-tō-san wa shinsetsu desu. お父さんは親切です。	Your father is kind.

Note that adjectival nominatives function here like the adjectives in Sentence Patterns 16 and 16A. Since adjectival nominatives do not conjugate, however, the past tense and the negative form are made with the appropriate forms of **desu** that you have already learned.

Past Tense

Kirei desu.	It is pretty.
きれいです。	
Kirei deshita.	It was pretty.
きれいでした。	

Present Negative

Kirei desu.	It is pretty.
きれいです。	
Kirei ja arimasen.	It is not pretty.
きれいじゃありません。	

Past Negative

Kirei desu.	It is pretty.
きれいです。	
Kirei ja arimasen deshita.	It was not pretty.
きれいじゃありませんでした。	

Sentence Pattern 19 shows how the particle **na** is always placed between an adjectival nominative and the noun it modifies.

Sentence Pattern 19	
ADJECTIVE NOMINATIVE + **na** + NOUN + **desu.** ADJECTIVE NOMINATIVE + な + NOUN + です。	It's a + ADJECTIVE+ NOUN.
TOPIC + **wa** / + ADJECTIVE NOMINATIVE + **na** + NOUN + **desu.** TOPIC + は + ADJECTIVE NOMINATIVE + な + NOUN + です。	TOPIC is a + ADJECTIVE+ NOUN.

Kirei na kōto desu. きれいなコートです。	It's a beautiful coat.
Suteki na reinkōto desu. 素敵なレインコートです。	It's a wonderful raincoat.
Yūmei na eiga desu. 有名な映画です。	It's a famous movie.
Taikutsu na hon desu. 退屈な本です。	It's a boring book.
Shizuka na resutoran desu. 静かなレストランです。	It's a quiet restaurant.
Suki na kēki desu. 好きなケーキです。	It's a cake that I like.
Kirai na hito desu. 嫌いな人です。	It's a person I dislike.
Dame na hito desu. だめな人です。	He (she) is a hopeless (no good) person.
Jōzu na Nihongo desu. 上手な日本語です。	It's well-spoken Japanese.
Heta na Nihongo desu. 下手な日本語 です。	It's poorly spoken Japanese.
Tanaka-san wa genki na hito desu. 田中さんは元気な人です。	Mr .Tanaka is a healthy person.
Yamada Sensei wa hima na hito desu. 山田先生は暇な人です。	Professor Yamada is a person with lots of free time.
O-tō-san wa shinsetsu na hito desu. お父さんは親切な人です。	Your father is a very kind person.

Practice

Practice repeating the following sentences aloud.

1. Talking about the weather

Kyō wa suteki na o-tenki desu ne. 今日は素敵なお天気ですね。	It's wonderful weather today, isn't it?
Kyō wa shizuka na hi desu ne. 今日は静かな日ですね。	It's a quiet day today, isn't it?

2. Talking about restaurants

Yūmei na resutoran desu.　It's a famous restaurant.
有名なレストランです。

Shizuka na resutoran desu.　It's a quiet restaurant.
静かなレストランです。

Suki na o-sushiya desu.　It's a sushi shop that I like.
好きなお寿司屋です。

Kirai na shokudō desu.　It's an eating place that I
嫌いな食堂です。　don't like.

Suehiro wa suteki na resutoran desu.　Suehiro is a wonderful
末広は素敵なレストランです。　restaurant.

Den-en wa yūmei na kissaten desu.　Den-en is a famous coffee
田園は有名な喫茶店です。　shop.

Kono shokudō wa suki na shokudō desu.　This eating place is a
この食堂は好きな食堂です。　favorite of mine.

3. Talking about yourself

Kirai desu.　I don't like (it).
嫌いです。

Suki desu.　I like (it).
好きです。

Taikutsu desu.　I am bored.
退屈です。

Hima desu.　I have a lot of free time.
暇です。

4. Talking about people

Suteki na hito desu ne.　He (or she) is a wonderful person,
素敵な人ですね。　isn't he (or she)?

Shinsetsu na hito desu.　He (or she) is a kind person.
親切な人です。

Kirei na hito desu ne.　She is a pretty person, isn't she?
きれいな人ですね。

Determining Likes and Dislikes

In this lesson you learn how to use the adjectival nominals **suki**, **kirai**, **jozu**, and **heta** to express likes, dislikes, what someone is skillful at, and what someone is not skillful at. There are a few new vocabulary terms in the lesson.

Vocabulary

Chūgokugo	中国語	Chinese (language)
Doitsugo	ドイツ語	German (language)
Eigo	英語	English (language)
Furansugo	フランス語	French (language)
o-ryori	お料理	cooking
piano	ピアノ	piano
Supeingo	スペイン語	Spanish (language)

Culture and vocabulary notes

The suffix **-go** means "language." It is used in compounds together with the name of a country to mean the national language of that country. For example, adding **-go** to the end of Japanese word for China (**Chūgoku**) produces the Japanese word for the Chinese language (**Chūgokugo**).

Grammar

Sentence Patterns 19

TOPIC (PERSON) + **wa** / + NOUN + **ga** / **suki desu.**	PERSON + is fond of
TOPIC (PERSON) + は + NOUN + が好きです。	+ NOUN.
TOPIC (PERSON) + **wa** / + NOUN + **ga** / **kirai desu.**	PERSON + is not fond of
TOPIC (PERSON) + は + NOUN + が嫌いです。	+ NOUN.
TOPIC (PERSON) + **wa** / + NOUN + **ga** / **jōzu desu.**	PERSON + is good at
TOPIC (PERSON) + は + NOUN + が上手です。	+ NOUN.
TOPIC (PERSON) + **wa** / + NOUN + **ga** / **heta desu.**	PERSON + is poor at
TOPIC (PERSON) + は + NOUN + が下手です。	+ NOUN.

Examples

(**Watakushi wa**) **tenisu ga suki desu.** （私は）テニスが好きです。	I'm fond of tennis.
Tanaka-san wa gorufu ga kirai desu. 田中さんはゴルフが嫌いです。	Mr. Tanaka is not fond of golf.
Sumisu-san wa Doitsugo ga jōzu desu. スミスさんはドイツ語が上手です。	Mr. Smith is good at German.
(**Watakushi wa**) **Supeingo ga heta desu.** （私は）スペイン語が下手です。	I'm poor at Spanish.

Note the use of **wa** and **ga** above. **Wa**, as you learned, denotes the topic of the sentence–here, who is talking or being talked about. **Ga** is used here to show what that person is fond of, good at, etc.

If you use the interrogative word **nani** in place of the noun in Sentence Pattern 18A, you will be able to ask about another person's likes, dislikes, and abilities.

Sentence Patterns 18B

TOPIC (PERSON) + **wa** / **nani ga** / **suki desu ka?** TOPIC (PERSON) + は何が好きですか？	What is + PERSON + fond of?
TOPIC (PERSON) + **wa** / **nani ga** / **kirai desu ka?** TOPIC (PERSON) + は何が嫌いですか？	What is + PERSON + not fond of?
TOPIC (PERSON) + **wa** / **nani ga** / **jōzu desu ka?** TOPIC (PERSON) + は何が上手ですか？	What is + PERSON + good at?
TOPIC (PERSON) + **wa** / **nani ga** / **heta desu ka?** TOPIC (PERSON) + は + 何が下手です。	What is + PERSON + is poor at?

Examples

Anata wa nani ga suki desu ka? あなたは何が好きですか？	What are you fond of?
(**Watakushi wa**) **piano ga suki desu.** （私は）ピアノが好きです。	I'm fond of piano (playing).
Anata wa nani ga kirai desu ka? あなたは何が嫌いですか？	What are you not fond of?
(**Watakushi wa**) **o-sashimi ga kirai desu.** （私は）お刺身が嫌いです。	I'm not fond of **sashimi**.

Keiko-san wa nani ga jōzu desu ka? 恵子さんは何が上手ですか？	What is Keiko good at?
Keiko-san wa o-ryōri ga jōzu desu. 恵子さんはお料理が上手です。	Keiko is good at cooking.
Anata wa nani ga heta desu ka? あなたは何が下手ですか？	What are you poor at?
(Watakushi wa) Eigo ga heta desu. （私は）英語が下手です。	I'm poor at English.

Practice

1. Answer the following questions using the word in parentheses. Turn to page 237 for answers.

   (a) Anata wa nani ga suki desu ka?　　　(tenpura)
       あなたは何が好きですか？　　　　（天ぷら）

   (b) Tanaka-san wa nani ga kirai desu ka?　(o-sake)
       田中さんは何が嫌いですか？　　　（お酒）

   (c) O-kā-san wa nani ga jōzu desu ka?　　(o-ryōri)
       お母さんは何が上手ですか？　　　（お料理）

   (d) O-tō-san wa nani ga jōzu desu ka?　　(Eigo)
       お父さんは何が上手ですか？　　　（英語）

   (e) Anata wa nani ga heta desu ka?　　　(piano)
       あなたは何が下手ですか？　　　　（ピアノ）

2. Change the following sentences into the negative. Turn to page 237 for answers.

   (a) Kirei desu.
       きれいです。

   (b) Kyōto e ikitai desu.
       京都へ行きたいです。

   (c) Omoshiroi desu.
       おもしろいです。

   (d) Watakushi wa Nihongo ga suki desu.
       私は日本語が好きです。

   (e) Tanoshii eiga deshita.
       楽しい映画でした。

(f) **Satō-san wa genki na hito desu.**
佐藤さんは元気な人です。

(g) **Tōkyō wa shizuka desu.**
東京は静かです。

(h) **Are wa yūbinkyoku desu.**
あれは郵便局です。

(i) **Sono kamera wa yasukatta desu.**
そのカメラは安かったです。

(j) **Yūmei na hito deshita.**
有名な人でした。

3. Make up your own answers to the following questions. Turn to page 237 for sample answers.

(a) **Nani ga tabetai desu ka?**
何が食べたいですか？

(b) **Nani ga nomitai desu ka?**
何が飲みたいですか？

(c) **Doko e ikitai desu ka?**
どこへ行きたいですか？

(d) **O-kā-san wa nani ga jōzu desu ka?**
お母さんは何が上手ですか？

(f) **Nani ga heta desu ka?**
何が下手ですか？

(g) **Nani ga kirai desu ka?**
何が嫌いですか？

Chapter 6
(Lessons 22 – 27)

Sentence Patterns Covered in Chapter 6	
Sentence Pattern 20	TOPIC + **wa** / **ikura desu ka?** TOPIC + は いくらですか？ (TOPIC + **wa**) / + AMOUNT + **desu.** (TOPIC + は) + AMOUNT + です。
Sentence Pattern 21	CATEGORY / + NUMBER-**mai** (**kudasai**). CATEGORY + NUMBER-枚（ください）。
Sentence Pattern 21A	DESTINATION + TYPE OF TICKET / + NUMBER-**mai** (**kudasai**). DESTINATION + TYPE OF TICKET + NUMBER-枚（ください）。
Sentence Pattern 21B	ITEM + **o** / + NUMBER-**mai kudasai.** ITEM + を + NUMBER-枚ください。
Sentence Pattern 22	Ima / nanji desu ka? 今何時ですか？ TIME + **desu.** TIME + です。
Sentence Pattern 23	Nanji ni + NOUN + **ga** / + VERB-INFINITIVE + -**tai desu ka?** 何時に + NOUN + が + VERB-INFINITIVE + たいですか？ Nanji ni + PLACE + **e** / **ikitai desu ka?** 何時に + PLACE + へ行きたいですか？
Sentence Pattern 24	(Anata no) denwa bangō wa / nanban desu ka? （あなたの）電話番号は何番ですか？ San kyū roku ichi no kyū san ichi ichi desu. 3961-9311です。

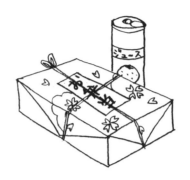

Dialogue
電車の駅で:
義広 ： 京都へ行きたいですが、切符はいくらですか？
駅員 ： 切符は一枚ですか？
義広 ： はい、そうです。
駅員 ： 京都までの切符は6,000円です。
義広 ： 電車は何時ですか？
駅員 ： 三時です。
義広 ： では一枚お願いします。

駅のプラットホームのキオスクで:
義広 ： これはいくらですか？
店員 ： お弁当ですか？800円です。
義広 ： それから、ジュースはいくらですか？
店員 ： ジュースは100円です。
義広 ： じゃあ、ジュースとお弁当を下さい。
店員 ： 全部で900円です。
義広 ： はい、1000円です。
店員 ： はい、お釣りは100円です。
　　　　ありがとうございます。
義広 ： ありがとう。

At a train station:

Yoshihiro	:	Kyōto e ikitai desu ga, kippu wa ikura desu ka?	I want to go to Kyoto but, how much does a ticket cost?
Attendant	:	Kippu wa ichimai desu ka?	One ticket?
Yoshihiro	:	Hai, sō desu.	Yes, that's right.
Attendant	:	Kyōto made no kippu wa rokusen-en desu.	A ticket to Kyoto costs 6,000 yen.
Yoshihiro	:	Densha wa nanji desu ka?	What time is the train?
Attendant	:	San-ji desu.	It's at 3 o'clock.
Yoshihiro	:	Dewa ichimai onegai shimasu.	Then, one (ticket) please.

At a kiosk on the train platform:

Yoshihiro	:	Kore wa ikura desu ka?	How much does this cost?
Clerk	:	O-bento desu ka? Happyaku-en desu.	An **o-bento** box? It costs 800 yen.
Yoshihiro	:	Sore kara, jusu wa ikura desu ka?	Also, how much does a juice cost?
Clerk	:	Jusu wa hyaku-en desu.	Juice costs 100 yen.
Yoshihiro	:	Jā, jusu to o-bentō o kudasai.	Okay, please give me a juice and an **o-bento** box.
Clerk	:	Zenbu de kyuhyaku-en desu.	All together that's 900 yen.
Yoshihiro	:	Hai, sen en desu.	Okay, here's 1,000 yen.
Clerk:	:	Hai, o-tsuri wa hyaku en desu. Arigatō gozaimasu.	Here, your change is 100 yen. Thank you very much.
Yoshihiro	:	Arigatō.	Thank you.

Dialogue vocabulary

Arigatō gozaimasu.	ありがとうございます。	Thank you.
dōzo	どうぞ	please (offering something)
dewa	では	then, / well then / ok
-en	円	yen
ga	が	but
hyaku	百	100
ichimai	一枚	one (flat object)
ikura	いくら	How much?
kippu	切符	ticket
made	まで	to/up to
nanji	何時	What time?
o-bentō	お弁当	a Japanese box lunch
Onegai shimasu.	お願いします。	Please help me (please do me a favor).
o-tsuri	お釣り	change (money)
san-ji	三時	3 o'clock
sen	千	1,000
zenbu de	全部で	all together; in total

Culture and vocabulary notes

This dialogue includes several fixed phrases that are extermely common in polite Japanese conversation. The expression **Onegai shimasu** can be used to try to gain someone's attention or as a more general request for help. **Arigatō gozaimasu** is a polite way to say *thank you*. You will learn some different ways to say *thank you* (some more informal and some more polite) later in the book. A common polite response to **Arigatō gozaimasu** is **Dō itashimashite**, meaning *You're welcome* or *Think nothing of it*. The word **dōzo** is commonly translated as *please*, meaning *Please take this*.

Numbers

This chapter is all about numbers and the situations in which they are most often used. Here you will be counting your money, picking up tickets at a theater or train station, buying postcards to send home, and keeping track of the time so you don't miss out on that concert, that Kabuki play, or that special tour bus headed for Kyoto. You'll also be learning about phone numbers in Japan; these will be useful when making reservations or when calling friends to say goodbye and thank them for the wonderful time you've had. Since numbers are so important, do your best to memorize the list below before studying Lesson 22.

Vocabulary

1	ichi	一	21	nijūichi	二十一	
2	ni	二	22	nijūni	二十二	
3	san	三	23	nijūsan	二十三	
4	shi (yo, yon)	四	24	nijūshi	二十四	
5	go	五	25	nijūgo	二十五	
6	roku	六	30	sanjū	三十	
7	shichi (nana)	七	40	yonjū	四十	
8	hachi	八	50	gojū	五十	
9	ku (kyū)	九	60	rokujū	六十	
10	jū	十	70	nanajū (shichijū)	七十	
11	jūichi	十一	80	hachijū	八十	
12	jūni	十二	90	kyūjū	九十	
13	jūsan	十三	100	hyaku	百	
14	jūshi (juyon)	十四	1,000	sen	千	
15	jūgo	十五	2,000	nisen	二千	
16	jūroku	十六	10,000	ichiman	一万	
17	jūshichi (jūnana)	十七	20,000	niman	二万	
18	jūhachi	十八	100,000	jūman	十万	
19	jūku (jūkyū)	十九	1,000,000	hyakuman	百万	
20	nijū	二十	100 million	oku	億	

Handling Money

The unit of Japanese currency is the yen, which in Japanese is pronounced **en** (円). Japanese numbers combine with the suffix **-en** to express amounts of money, just as in English we say "two dollars," "twelve dollars," etc.

Vocabulary

o-kane	お金	money	**-satsu**	札	bill
-en	円	yen	**ikura**	いくら	How much?
-dama	玉	coin			

ichi-en	¥1	**nanahyaku-en**	¥700
ni-en	¥2	**happyaku-en**	¥800
san-en	¥3	***kyūhyaku-en**	¥900
***yo-en**	¥4	**sen-en**	¥1,000
go-en	¥5	**nisen-en**	¥2,000
roku-en	¥6	**sanzen-en**	¥3,000
shichi-en (nana-en)	¥7	***yonsen-en**	¥4,000
hachi-en	¥8	**gosen-en**	¥5,000
***kyū-en**	¥9	**rokusen-en**	¥6,000
jū-en	¥10	**nanasen-en**	¥7,000
nijū-en	¥20	**hassen-en**	¥8,000
sanjū-en	¥30	***kyūsen-en**	¥9,000
***yonjū-en**	¥40	**ichiman-en**	¥10,000
gojū-en	¥50	**niman-en**	¥20,000
rokūjū-en	¥60	**sanman-en**	¥30,000
nanajū-en	¥70	***yonman-en**	¥40,000
hachijū-en	¥80	**goman-en**	¥50,000
kyūjū-en	¥90	**rokuman-en**	¥60,000
hyaku-en	¥100	**nanaman-en**	¥70,000
nihyaku-en	¥200	**hachiman-en**	¥80,000
sanbyaku-en	¥300	***kyūman-en**	¥90,000
***yonhyaku-en**	¥400	**jūman-en**	¥100,000
gohyaku-en	¥500	**hyakuman-en**	¥1,000,000
roppyaku-en	¥600		

Culture and vocabulary notes

An asterisk in the above list means that some forms of the number in question, as shown in the list near the beginning of this chapter, cannot be used for counting money. In some situations where numbers are used, alternate forms must be used. And sometimes either form will do. Since there are no firm rules concerning this, study carefully the usages given throughout this chapter.

Notice that the Japanese count higher numbers in units of ten thousand (**-man**). Therefore, 100,000 is **jūman**, or 10 ten-thousands, and 1,000,000 is **hyakuman**, or 100 ten-thousands. Also note that prices are usually written in Japanese using Arabic numerals rather than kanji.

Japanese words beginning with the numbers **san-**, **roku-**, and **hachi-** often show slight sound modifications. Look at these: **sanbyaku**, **roppyaku**, **happyaku**, **sanzen**, **hassen**.

Grammar

Sentence Pattern 20

TOPIC + **wa** / **ikura desu ka?** TOPIC + はいくらですか？	How much is + TOPIC?
(TOPIC + **wa**) / + AMOUNT + **desu.** (TOPIC + は) + AMOUNT + です。	It's + AMOUNT.

Examples

Kore wa ikura desu ka?
これははいくらですか？ — How much is this?

(Sore wa) nisen-en desu.
（それは）2,000円です。 — That (by you) is ¥2,000.

Kono kamera wa ikura desu ka?
このカメラはいくらですか？ — How much is this camera?

(Sore wa) sanman-en desu.
（それは）30,000円です。 — That (by you) is ¥30,000.

Ano sētā wa ikura desu ka?
あのセーターはいくらですか？ — How much is that sweater (over there)?

(Ano sētā wa) yonsen-gohyaku-en desu.
（あのセーターは）4,500円です。 — That (over there) is ¥4,500.

Sono kōtō wa ikura desu ka?
そのコートーはいくらですか？ — How much is that coat (by you)?

(Kore wa) ichiman-nisen-en desu.   This is ¥12,000.
（これは）12,000円です。

Note the similarity of this pattern to Sentence Pattern 8 in Chapter 3. The topic here can be a single word like **kore** or any modified noun.

When specifying amounts of money, simply combine the numbers you have learned and add the word for yen, **-en**, to the last number.

210円	**nihyaku-jū-en**
360円	**sanbyaku-rokujū-en**
1,540円	**sen-gohyaku-yonjū-en**
3,295円	**sanzen-nihyaku-kyūjū-go-en**
12,450円	**ichiman-nisen-yonhyaku-gojū-en**

Practice

1. Say the following amounts in Japanese. Turn to page 237 for answers.

(a)	¥20	(e)	¥445	(i)	¥3,500	(m)	¥37,899
(b)	¥90	(f)	¥670	(j)	¥6,890	(n)	¥62,355
(c)	¥100	(g)	¥1,250	(k)	¥8,625		
(d)	¥350	(h)	¥2,360	(l)	¥10,500		

2. Translate the following questions into Japanese. Turn to page 237 for answers.

   (a) How much is this?
   (b) How much is that radio?
   (c) How much is this stereo?
   (d) How much is the full-course dinner?

3. Practice the following:

¥10,000 bill	**ichiman-en-satsu**	10,000円札
¥5,000 bill	**gosen-en-satsu**	5,000円札
¥1,000 bill	**sen-en-satsu**	1,000円札
¥500 coin	**gohyaku-en-dama**	500円玉
¥100 coin	**hyaku-en-dama**	100円玉
¥50 coin	**gojū-en-dama**	50円玉
¥10 coin	**jū-en-dama**	10円玉
¥5 coin	**go-en-dama**	5円玉
¥1 coin	**ichi-en-dama**	1円玉

Buying Tickets at a Movie Theater

In this lesson you will learn how to purchase tickets using the counter for thin, flat objects.

Vocabulary

gakusei	学生	student
kippu	切符	ticket
kodomo	子供	child
otona	大人	adult

Grammar

Sentence Pattern 21	
CATEGORY / + NUMBER-**mai (kudasai)** CATEGORY + NUMBER-枚 (ください)。	(Please give me) + NUMBER + CATEGORY (of tickets).

Examples

Otona, ichi-mai (kudasai).　(Please) give me one adult ticket.
大人、一枚ください。

Kodomo, ni-mai (kudasai).　(Please) give me two children's tickets.
子供、一枚ください。

This sentence pattern is basically the same as Sentence Pattern 1. Notice that **kudasai** is often omitted; when buying tickets the important thing is to finish quickly. This part of Japanese life is even more fast-paced than it is in the United States.

The suffix -**mai** is what we will call a counter. A counter is a word that attaches to or follows a number to show the type or class of the item being counted. For thin, flat things, in English one would use the counter "sheets." For example, one would say, "three sheets of typing paper." For edible things bought in bulk, the counter "pounds" is often used, as in "five pounds of potatoes" or "two pounds of flour." Japanese has many such counters. Here the counter -**mai** refers to thin, flat objects like tickets, pamphlets, or paper. Since it is obvious at the ticket window what kind of thin, flat thing you are requesting, you need not use the word **kippu** for "ticket."

First you specify the kind of ticket (adult, student, child) and then the number of tickets that you want. When buying more than one kind of ticket—for example, one ticket for an adult and one for a child—simply combine the patterns:

Otona, ichi-mai; kodomo, ichi-mai.

Notice that in Japanese the type of thing you want is specified first and then the quantity that you want—just the reverse of the way it is done in English.

Practice
Try buying tickets for the following. Turn to page 237 for answers.
1. One adult
2. Two students
3. Two adults
4. Three children, one adult
5. Two adults, one student, two children
6. One student, three children.

Buying Tickets at a Train Station

In this lesson you will learn how to purchase various types of train tickets using the counter **-mai**.

Vocabulary

kaisūken	回数券	coupon ticket
katamichi (kippu)	片道	one-way (ticket)
kenbaiki	券売機	ticket-selling machine
kippu uriba	切符売り場	ticket window
made	～まで	to, up to, as far as
ōfuku (kippu)	往復	round-trip (ticket)

Culture and vocabulary notes

If you are in a train station in a large city and are not planning to travel a great distance, try buying your ticket at an automatic ticket-selling machine *(kenbaiki)*. Above the machine there is usually a chart showing the fares to various destinations. Since most of these charts show the station names in **kanji**, try, before you set out, to learn the characters used in the name of the place you are going. If you have any problems, find a station employee and ask:

DESTINATION **made ikura desu ka?**
Tōkyō Eki made ikura desu ka?
東京駅までいくらですか?
How much does it cost to Tokyo Station?

Made means "to" or "up to" or "as far as." Let us suppose that the station employee tells you that the fare is ¥130. Look for a machine that sells tickets of that amount. Since these machines make change, insert the exact amount, ¥150, or ¥200. If you have to use a machine that sells tickets of more than one price, insert your coins and push the button marked ¥130. If you plan to make the same trip often, it's cheaper to buy **kaisūken**, coupon tickets.

Grammar

Sentence Pattern 21A	
DESTINATION / TYPE OF TICKET / + NUMBER-**mai (kudasai)** DESTINATION / TYPE OF TICKET / + NUMBER-枚（ください）。	(Please) give me + number + (of tickets) of + CATEGORY + to + DESTINATION.

Examples

Yokohama, gakusei, ichi-mai.
横浜、学生、一枚。

A student ticket to Yokohama.

Shibuya, ni-mai.
渋谷、二枚。

Two tickets to Shibuya.

Kōbe, ōfuku, san-mai.
神戸、往復、三枚。

Three round-trip tickets to Kobe.

Kyōto, katamichi; otona, ni-mai; kodomo, ichi-mai.
京都、片道、大人、二枚、
子供一枚。

Two adult and one child one-way tickets to Kyoto.

Kōbe, ōfuku, ichi-mai.
神戸、往復、一枚。

A round-trip ticket to Kobe.

When buying train tickets at a ticket window, always give your destination first. Then specify the type of ticket (round-trip, adult, etc.) and the number of tickets, using the counter -**mai**. If you don't specify **gakusei** or **kodomo**, the ticket seller will assume that you want an adult ticket.

Practice

Translate the following questions into Japanese. Turn to page xxx for answers.

1. A student ticket to Sapporo, please.
2. One (adult) round-trip ticket to Nara, please.
3. Two (adult) one-way tickets to Tokyo, please.
4. One adult, two student, and one child round-trip tickets to Kyoto, please.
5. Two (adult) round-trip tickets to Kamakura, please.

Buying Tickets at the Post Office

In this lesson you will learn how to use the counter –**mai** to purchase a variety of thin, flat items.

Vocabulary

hagaki	はがき	postcard
hankachi	ハンカチ	handkerchief
kitte	切手	stamp
kōkūshokan	航空書簡	aerogram
sukāfu	スカーフ	scarf

Culture and vocabulary notes

The counter -**mai** is used not only for tickets but for stamps, postcards, and aerograms. This same counter can be used for many other items that are flat and thin, such as handkerchiefs, scarves, kimonos (because they become flat and thin when folded!), dishes, newspapers, sheets, blankets, and so on.

Grammar

Sentence Pattern 21B	
ITEM + o / + NUMBER-**mai kudasai.** ITEM + o + NUMBER-枚ください。	Please give me + NUMBER + ITEM.

Examples

Nijū-en kitte o go-mai kudasai. 20円切手を五枚ください。	Please give me five ¥20 stamps.
Hyaku-nijū-en kitte o jū-mai kudasai. 120円切手を十枚ください。	Please give me ten ¥120 stamps.
Hagaki o go-mai kudasai. はがきを五枚ください。	Please give me five postcards.
Kōkūshokan o ichi-mai kudasai. 航空書簡を一枚ください。	Please give me one aerogram.

The number plus -**mai** follows the particle **o**. When buying more than one kind of item you can use the particle **to**, "and."

Nijū-en kitte o go-mai to hagaki o
  jū-mai kudasai.
20円切手を五枚とはがきを
  十枚ください。

Please give me five ¥20 stamps
  and ten postcards.

Kōkūshokan o jū-mai to hagaki o
  go-mai kudasai.
航空書簡を十枚とはがきを
  五枚ください。

Please give me ten aerograms
  and five postcards.

The following sentences show other examples of the use of the counter -**mai**. Notice in the last example that the -**tai desu** construction can be used in place of **kudasai**.

Kono hankachi o ichi-mai kudasai.
このハンカチを一枚ください。

Please give me one of these
  handkerchiefs.

Kono hankachi o san-mai kudasai.
このハンカチを三枚ください。

Please give me three of these
  handkerchiefs.

Ano sukāfu o ichi-mai kudasai.
あのスカーフを一枚ください。

Please give me one of those
  scarves.

Ano sukāfu o ni-mai kudasai.
あのスカーフを二枚ください。

Please give me two of those
  scarves.

Kimono o ichi-mai kaitai desu.
着物を一枚買いたいです。

I'd like to buy one kimono.

Practice

1. Ask for the following items. Turn to page 238 for answers.
   (a) Five postcards
   (b) Ten aerograms
   (c) Five ¥20 stamps
   (d) Twenty ¥80 stamps
   (e) Four ¥120 stamps
   (f) Five ¥80 stamps and ten postcards
   (g) Twenty ¥20 stamps and five aerograms

Keeping Track of the Time

In this lesson you will how to express the time in hours and minutes and how to ask what time it is.

Vocabulary

-fun- (pun)	～分	minutes
-han	～半	half hour
ima	今	now
-ji	～時	-o'clock
mae	前	before
nanji	何時	What time?

Hour

1:00	ichi-ji	一時
2:00	ni-ji	二時
3:00	san-ji	三時
4:00	*yo-ji	四時
5:00	go-ji	五時
6:00	roku-ji	六時
7:00	shichi-ji (nana-ji)	七時
8:00	hachi-ji	八時
9:00	* ku-ji	九時
10:00	jū-ji	十時
11:00	jūichi-ji	十一時
12:00	jūni-ji	十二時

Half-Hour

1:30	ichi-ji-han	一時半
2:30	ni-ji-han	二時半
3:30	san-ji-han	三時半
4:30	* yo-ji-han	四時半
5:30	go-ji-han	五時半
6:30	roku-ji-han	六時半
7:30	shichi-ji-han (nana-ji-han)	七時半
8:30	hachi-ji-han	八時半
9:30	* ku-ji-han	九時半
10:30	jū-ji-han	十時半
11:30	jūichi-ji-han	十一時半
12:30	jūni-ji-han	十二時半

Culture and vocabulary notes

An asterisk in the preceding chart means that the number's alternate form (as given in the list on page 139), cannot be used here.

Notice that the suffix -han, which means "half past the hour," is attached after the -ji for "o'clock." In talking about train time, a 24-hour clock is used to avoid confusion:

13:00	jūsan-ji	十三時
14:00	*jūyo-ji	十四時
15:00	jūgo-ji	十五時
16:00	jūroku-ji	十六時
17:00	jūshichi-ji (jūnana-ji)	十七時
18:00	jūhachi-ji	十八時
19:00	jūku-ji (jūkyū-ji)	十九時
20:00	nijū-ji	二十時
21:00	nijūichi-ji	二十一時
22:00	nijūni-ji	二十二時
23:00	nijūsan-ji	二十三時
24:00	*nijūyo-ji	二十四時

Grammar

1. Finding the Time

The following sentence pattern is the one most frequently used for asking the time of day.

Sentence Pattern 22	
Ima / nanji desu ka? 今何時ですか？	What time is it now?
TIME + **desu.** TIME + です。	It's + TIME.

To give the exact number of minutes after the hour, use the numbers you have learned plus the counter -**fun**. Note the sound changes in the list below.

ippun	一分	1 minute
ni-fun	二分	2 minutes
san-pun	三分	3 minutes
*yon-pun	四分	4 minutes
go-fun	五分	5 minutes
roppun	六分	6 minutes
shichi-fun (nana-fun)	七分	7 minutes
hachi-fun (happun)	八分	8 minutes
*kyū-fun	九分	9 minutes
juppun (jippun)	十分	10 minutes

Minutes are combined with hours to give the exact time of day.

ni-ji	+	go-fun	→	ni-ji go-fun
二時		五分		二時五分
2 o'clock		5 minutes		2:05

go-ji	+	nijugo-fun	→	goji nijūgo-fun
五時		二十五分		五時二十五分
5 o'clock		25 minutes		5:25

Just as you can say "20 before 8" instead of "7:40," Japanese sometimes use the word **mae**, "before," to make a similar statement:

shichi-ji	+	yonjuppun	→	shichi-ji yonjuppun
七時		40分		七時四十分
7 o'clock		40 minutes		7:40

[or]

hachi-ji	–	nijuppun	→	hachi-ji nijuppun mae
八時		二十分		八時二十分前
8 o'clock		20 minutes		20 minutes before 8

jūichi-ji	+	gojūgo-fun	→	jūichi-ji gojūgo-fun
十一時		五十五分		十一時五十五分
11 o'clock		55 minutes		11:55

[or]

jūni-ji	–	go-fun	→	jūni-ji go-fun mae
十二時		五分		十二時五分前
12 o'clock		5 minutes		5 minutes before 12

2. Finding out "At what Time?"

Using **nanji**, "what time?" you will be able to find out what time something is going to happen.

Sentence Pattern 23

Nanji ni + NOUN + **ga** / + VERB-INFINITIVE + **-tai desu ka?**	At what time would you like to + VERB + NOUN?
何時に + NOUN + が + VERB-INFINITIVE + たいですか？	

Nanji ni + PLACE + e / ikitai desu ka? 何時に+ PLACE + へ行きたいですか？	At what time would you like to go to + PLACE?

Examples

Nanji ni gohan ga tabetai desu ka?
何時にご飯が食べたいですか？

At what time would you like to eat?

Ichi-ji ni tabetai desu.
一時に食べたいです。

I'd like to eat at 1:00.

Nanji ni Kyōto e ikitai desu ka?
何時に京都へ行きたいですか？

At what time would you like to go to Kyoto?

San-ji ni ikitai desu.
三時に行きたいです。

I'd like to go at 3:00.

The particle **ni** is used here to denote a specific time. This pattern can also be used with other verb-forms you have learned.

Nanji ni gohan o tabemashō ka?
何時にごはんを食べましょうか？

At what time shall we eat?

Ichi-ji ni tabemashō.
一時に食べましょう。

Let's eat at 1:00.

Practice

1. Practice Sentence Pattern 22, answering with the following times. Turn to page 238 for answers.

   (a) 4:00
   (b) 7:00
   (c) 11:30
   (d) 6:30
   (e) 2:15
   (f) 3:15
   (g) 11:00
   (h) 9:30
   (i) 10:30

   (j) 4:36
   (k) 5:29
   (l) 1:07
   (m) 6:00
   (n) 8:30
   (o) 12:38
   (p) 6:47
   (q) 4:45
   (r) 5:31

   (s) 1:30
   (t) 7:50
   (u) 8:55
   (v) 2:30
   (w) 3:34
   (x) 10:13
   (y) 11:35

2. Answer the following questions. Turn to page 238 for sample answers.

   (a) **Nanji ni yūbinkyoku e ikimashō ka?**
   (b) **Nanji ni gohan o tabemashō ka?**
   (c) **Nanji ni yūbinkyoku e ikitai desu ka?**

Understanding Telephone Numbers

In this lesson you will learn how to understand phone numbers in Japanese.

Vocabulary

bangō	番号	number
denwa	電話	telephone
maru	0 / まる	zero
Nanban?	何番？	What number?
rei	0 / 零	zero
zero	0 / ゼロ	zero

Culture and vocabulary notes

Denwa bangō means "phone number." A literal translation of the first sample sentence below might be "What is the number of your phone number?" Though this seems redundant in English, such phrasing is not unusual in Japanese. Note that English uses a pause to denote the hyphen break in the written number, while Japanese uses the particle **no**.

Each number in a telephone number should be spoken with equal stress and duration, though you may sometimes hear the numbers 2, **ni**, and 5, **go**, lengthened to **nii** and **gō**. Because **shichi** and **ichi** sound alike, **nana** is most often used for 7. The number "0" can be pronounced **zero**, **rei**, or **maru**. **Maru** can also mean "circle" or "money," but different kanji are used in those cases, and the correct meaning can be inferred from the context. It seems to be the preferred word for *zero* among many merchants.

For example, 671-0302 may be pronounced three ways:

roku nana ichi no ⎰ zero san zero ni
⎱ rei san rei ni
⎱ maru san maru ni

The discussion above refers to how Japanese phone numbers are pronounced. They are typically written using Arabic numerals, not kanji.

Grammar

Sentence Pattern 24	
(Anata no) denwa bangō wa / nanban desu ka? （あなたの）電話番号は何番ですか？	What is your telephone number?
San kyū roku ichi no kyū san ichi ichi desu. 3961-9311です。	It's 3961-9311.

Practice

1. Practice saying these telephone numbers in Japanese. Turn to page 238 see the answers.

   (a) 3771-7910

   (b) 3631-2661

   (c) 3757-5411

   (d) 3261-0061

   (e) 3961-9340

   (f) 3805-9471

2. Practice saying these telephone numbers in Japanese. Note that telephone numbers in rural areas often begin with two digits. Turn to page 238 for the answers.

   (a) 66-3784

   (b) 23-0871

   (c) 32-3672

   (d) 23-4838

Chapter 7
(Lessons 28 – 30)

Sentence Patterns Covered in Chapter 7	
Sentence Pattern 25	VERB-INFINITIVE + -**masu.** VERB-INFINITIVE + ます。
Sentence Pattern 26	VERB-INFINITIVE + -**mashita.** VERB-INFINITIVE + ました。
Sentence Pattern 27	VERB-INFINITIVE + -**masen deshita.** VERB-INFINITIVE + ませんでした。

This chapter introduces a simple but important verb-form that will enable you to describe your habits, your plans, and the things you have, or haven't, experienced in Japan. The chapter has been designed to get you using this verb form as soon as possible, for you will use it often. The more complicated details appear at the end of the chapter in a special explanatory lesson; read through this lesson for general understanding when you come to it, but don't feel that you have to memorize it before moving on in the book. Instead, review and practice the material here often so that you feel comfortable with it.

Dialogue
幸子 ： 昨日は何をしましたか？
由美 ： 昨日は友達と京都へ行きました。
幸子 ： 京都で何をしましたか？

由美 ： 朝、清水寺を見ました。それからレストランで昼ご
　　　　飯を食べました。
幸子 ： 何を食べましたか？
由美 ： 私はそばを食べました。友達はピザを食べました。
幸子 ： 金閣寺も見ましたか？
由美 ： いいえ、見ませんでした。昼ご飯の後ちょっと買い
　　　　物をしました。
幸子 ： 何を買いましたか？
由美 ： ブラウスを買いました。
幸子 ： それから家に帰りましたか？
由美 ： いいえ、とても暑かったから沢山アイスクリームを
　　　　食べました。昨日の晩京都駅まで行きました。
幸子 ： 今日は何をしますか？
由美 ： 家で休みます。

Sachiko	: **Kinō wa nani o shimashita ka?**	What did you do yesterday?
Yumi	: **Kinō wa tomodachi to Kyōto e ikimashita.**	Yesterday I went with my friend to Kyoto.
Sachiko	: **Kyōto de nani o shimashita ka?**	What did you do in Kyoto?
Yumi	: **Asa Kiyomizu-dera o mimashita. Sore kara resutoran de hirugohan o tabemashita.**	We visited Kiyomizu Temple in the morning. After that we ate lunch at a restaurant.
Sachiko	: **Nani o tabemashita ka?**	What did you eat?
Yumi	: **Watashi wa soba o tabemashita. Tomodachi wa pizza o tabemashita.**	I ate soba noodles and my friend ate pizza.
Sachiko	: **Kinkaku-ji mo mimashita ka?**	Did you also see the Golden Pavilion Temple?
Yumi	**Iie, mimasen deshita. Hirugohan no ato chotto kaimono o shimashita.**	No, we didn't see it. After lunch we did some shopping.
Sachiko	: **Nani o kaimashita ka?**	What did you buy?
Yumi	: **Burausu o kaimashita.**	I bought a blouse.
Sachiko	: **Sore kara uchi ni kaerimashita ka?**	Did you return home after that?

Yumi	: Iie, totemo atsukatta kara, takusan aisu kuriimu o tabe-mashita. Kinō no ban Kyōto eki made ikimashita.	No, it was very hot, so we ate a lot of ice cream. Then we went to Kyoto station last night.
Sachiko:	Kyō wa nani o shimasu ka?	What will you do today?
Yumi:	Uchi de yasumimasu.	I'll rest at home.

Dialogue vocabulary

asa	朝	morning
ato	あと	after
atsukatta	暑かった	it was hot
burausu	ブラウス	blouse
hirugohan	昼ご飯	lunch
ikimashita	行きました	went
kaimashita	買いました	bought
Kinkaku-ji	金閣寺	the Golden Pavilion Temple
kinō	昨日	yesterday
Kiyomizu-dera	清水寺	Kiyomizu Temple
kyō	今日	today
mimasen deshita	見ませんでした	didn't see it
mimashita	見ました	saw (*v*)
piza	ピザ	pizza
shimasu	します	do; will do
takusan	沢山	a lot
totemo	とても	very
yasumimasu	休みます	rest; will rest

Telling What You Do or Will Do

In this lesson you will learn the common **–masu** form of Japanese verbs to express actions that regularly occur or will occur in the future. You will also learn vocabulary that will allow you to express when an action takes place: past, present, or future. Finally, you will also learn some words that will allow you to describe how frequently you perform an action.

Vocabulary

asatte	あさって	the day after tomorrow
ikimasu	行きます	to go
itsumo	いつも	always
kaimasu	買います	to buy
taitei	たいてい	usually
tokidoki	時々	sometimes
yoku	よく	frequently, often

Culture and vocabulary notes

Perhaps the -**masu** verb-form is the one you will be using most often in Japan. Verbs that end in -**masu** are always polite, and they indicate either present/habitual (the customary actions one engages in) or future (what will happen) time. Thus, if someone asks you **Unagi o tabemasu ka?**, he or she usually means "Do you eat eel?" or "Will you eat eel?"

These are the -**masu** forms of the action verbs you have learned so far:

ikimasu	行きます	go; will go
kaimasu	買います	buy; will buy
mimasu	見ます	see; will see
nomimasu	飲みます	drink; will drink
shimasu	します	do; will do
tabemasu	食べます	eat; will eat
yasumimasu	休みます	rest; will rest

Here are some words that can be used to express relative time, i.e, the past, present, or future:

Unit	Previous	This	Next	Every
Day	kinō 昨日	kyō 今日	ashita 明日	mainichi 毎日
Week	senshū 先週	konshū 今週	raishū 来週	maishū 毎週
Month	sengetsu 先月	kongetsu 今月	raigetsu 来月	maitsuki 毎月
Year	kyonen 去年	kotoshi 今年	rainen 来年	mainen (maitoshi) 毎年 (毎年)
Morning	kinō no asa 昨日の朝	kesa 今朝	ashita no asa 明日の朝	maiasa 毎朝
Evening	kinō no ban 昨日の晩	konban 今晩	ashita no ban 明日の晩	maiban 毎晩
Night	kinō no yoru 昨日の夜	kon-ya 今夜	ashita no yoru 明日の夜	maiyo 毎夜

Grammar

Sentence Pattern 25

VERB-INFINITIVE + -masu.	I (will) do + VERB.
VERB-INFINITIVE + -ます。	

Examples

Itsumo resutoran de biifusutēki o tabemasu.
いつもレストランでビーフステーキを食べます。

I always eat steak at a restaurant.

Mainichi Tōkyō e ikimasu.
毎日東京へ行きます。

I go to Tokyo every day.

Ashita resutoran de biifusutēki o tabemasu.
明日レストランでビーフステーキを食べます。

Tomorrow I'm going to eat steak at a restaurant.

Asatte Tōkyō e ikimasu.
あさって東京へ行きます。

I'm going to Tokyo the day after tomorrow.

The particle **ni** is not used with words like **ashita**, **raishū**, **itsumo**, etc. because these words do not show a specific point of time, as does **shichiji** or **goji**. The **de** in **resutoran de** above shows where the action takes place.

Practice
Practice saying the following conversations aloud.

Mainichi doko de gohan o tabemasu ka?　　Where do you eat every day?
毎日どこでごはんを食べますか？

Uchi de tabemasu.　　I eat at home.
うちで食べます。

Taitei nani o nomimasu ka?　　What do you usually drink?
たいてい何を飲みますか？

Biiru o nomimasu.　　I drink beer.
ビールを飲みます。

Tokidoki eiga e ikimasu ka?　　Do you sometimes go to the
時々映画へ行きますか？　　movies?

Hai, ikimasu.　　Yes, I do.
はい、行きます。

Konban nani o shimasu ka?　　What are you going to do
今晩何をしますか？　　tonight?

Eiga o mimasu.　　I will see a movie.
映画を見ます。

Konban doko de gohan o tabemasu ka?　　Where are you going to eat
今晩どこでごはんを食べますか？　　tonight?

Resutoran de tabemasu.　　I'm going to eat at a restaurant.
レストランで食べます。

Telling What You Did Do

In this lesson you will learn to use the polite past verb form, -**mashita**, to express an action that occurred in the past.

Vocabulary

ototoi	おととい	the day before yesterday
ototoshi	おととし	the year before last

Culture and vocabulary notes

In the last example sentence below, **Nihon no eiga o mimashita**, the particle **no** is used to make the noun **Nihon** (Japan) modify the noun **eiga** (movie), That is, it is used to explain what type of movie it is.

Grammar

Sentence Pattern 26	
VERB-INFINITIVE + -**mashita**.	I did + VERB.
VERB-INFINITIVE + ました。	

Examples

Kinō sukiyaki o tabemashita. 昨日すき焼きを食べました。	I ate sukiyaki yesterday.
Ototoi Kyōto e ikimashita. おととい京都へ行きました。	I went to Kyoto the day before yesterday.
Senshū terebi o kaimashita. 先週テレビを買いました。	I bought a television last week.
Ototoshi Kabuki o mimashita. おととし歌舞伎を見ました。	I saw a Kabuki play the year before last.
Kesa kōhii o nomimashita. 今朝コーヒーを飲みました。	I drank coffee this morning.
Nihon no eiga o mimashita. 日本の映画を見ました。	I saw a Japanese movie.

The polite past tense is formed by changing -**masu** to -**mashita**. The -**mashita** form indicates actions completed in the past.

ikimasu	ikimashita	nomimasu	nomimashita
行きます	行きました	飲みます	飲みました
kaimasu	kaimashita	shimasu	shimashita
買います	買いました	します	しました
mimasu	mimashita	tabemasu	tabemashita
見ます	見ました	食べます	食べました

Practice

1. Practice repeating the following dialogue aloud.

(Anata wa) kinō nani o shimashita ka?
（あなたは）昨日何をしましたか？
What did you do yesterday?

Ginza e ikimashita.
銀座へ行きました。
I went to the Ginza (a neighborhood of Tokyo.)

(Anata wa) ototoi nani o shimashita ka?
（あなたは）おととい何をしましたか？
What did you do the day before yesterday?

Eiga e ikimashita.
映画へ行きました。
I went to a movie.

Kinō doko de gohan o tabemashita ka?
昨日どこでご飯を食べましたか？
Where did you have meal yesterday?

Suehiro de tabemashita.
末広で食べました。
I ate at *Suehiro*.

Nani o tabemashita ka?
何を食べましたか？
What did you eat?

Biifusutēki to sarada o tabemashita.
ビーフステーキとサラダを食べました。
I ate a steak and salad.

Nani o mimashita ka?
何を見ましたか？
What did you see?

Amerika no eiga o mimashita.
アメリカの映画を見ました。
I saw an American movie.

2. In Japanese, ask these questions of yourself and make up answers to them. Turn to lessons 29 - 30 to see some sample answers.

    (a) What do you usually do?
    (b) What are you going to do tomorrow?
    (c) What are you going to do next week?
    (d) What are you going to do next year?
    (e) What did you do yesterday?
    (f) What did you do last month?
    (g) What did you buy yesterday?
    (h) Where did you buy that raincoat yesterday?
    (i) What did you see last night?
    (j) Where did you go yesterday?
    (k) What did you drink this morning?
    (1) Where do you usually eat?

3. Using the following words, make up sentences about some of your regular activities.

itsumo	tokidoki	taitei	yoku
いつも	時々	たいてい	よく

    Examples:

    Taitei uchi de gohan o tabemasu.　　　I usually eat at home.
    たいてい家でごはんを食べます。

    Mainichi ginkō e ikimasu.　　　I go to the bank every day.
    毎日銀行へ行きます。

4. Using the following words, make up sentences about some of your past activities.

kinō	sengetsu	ototoi	kyonen	senshū
昨日	先月	おととい	去年	先週

Examples:

Kinō sukiyaki o tabemashita.　　　I ate **sukiyaki** yesterday.
昨日すき焼きを食べました。

Senshū eiga o mimashita.　　　I saw a movie last week.
先週映画を見ました。

Telling What You Don't or Didn't Do

In this lesson you will learn to use the polite negative verb form, -**masen**, and the polite negative past verb form, -**masen deshita**. No new vocabulary is introduced.

Grammar

Sentence Pattern 27	
VERB-INFINITIVE + -**masen.** VERB-INFINITIVE + ません。	I don't (won't) + VERB.
VERB-INFINITIVE + -**masen deshita.** VERB-INFINITIVE + ませんでした。	I didn't + VERB.

Examples

Kyō Tōkyō e ikimasen.
今日東京へ行きません。

I'm not going to Tokyo today.

Kinō Tōkyō e ikimasen deshita.
昨日東京へ行きませんでした。

I didn't go to Tokyo yesterday.

Ashita uchi de tabemasen.
明日家で食べません。

I won't eat at home tomorrow.

Kinō sukiyaki o tabemasen deshita.
昨日すき焼きを食べませんでした。

I didn't eat **sukiyaki** yesterday.

Kesa kōhii o nomimasen deshita.
今朝コーヒーを飲みませんでした。

I didn't drink coffee this morning.

To form the polite negative present-habitual/future and the polite negative past, attach -**masen** and -**masen deshita** to the verb-infinitive.

present	past	negative	past negative
ikimasu	ikimashita	ikimasen	ikimasen deshita
行きます	行きました	行きません	行きませんでした
kaimasu	kaimashita	kaimasen	kaimasen deshita
買います	買いました	買いません	買いませんでした

mimasu	mimashita	mimasen	mimasen deshita
見ます	見ました	見ません	見ませんでした
nomimasu	nomimashita	nomimasen	nomimasen deshita
飲みます	飲みました	飲みません	飲みませんでした
shimasu	shimashita	shimasen	shimasen deshita
します	しました	しません	しませんでした
tabemasu	tabemashita	tabemasen	tabemasen deshita
食べます	食べました	食べません	食べませんでした

Practice

Practice repeating the following dialogue aloud.

Kyō eiga e ikimasu ka?
今日映画へ行きます？

Are you going to a movie today?

Iie, ikimasen.
いいえ、行きません。

No, I'm not.

Sono omoshiroi eiga o mimashita ka?
そのおもしろい映画を見ましたか？

Did you see that interesting movie?

Iie, mimasen deshita.
いいえ、見ませんでした。

No, I didn't.

Kinō depāto de kimono o kaimashita ka?
昨日デパートで着物を買いましたか？

Did you buy a kimono at the department store yesterday?

Iie, kaimasen deshita.
いいえ、買いませんでした。

No, I didn't.

Rainen Hawai e ikimasu ka?
来年ハワイへ行きますか？

Are you going to Hawaii next year?

Iie, ikimasen. Furansu e ikimasu.
いいえ、行きません。フランスへ行きます。

No, I'm not. I'm going to France.

Ashita tenisu o shimasu ka?
明日テニスをしますか？

Will you play tennis tomorrow?

Iie, shimasen. Gorufu o shimasu.
いいえ、しません。ゴルフをします。

No. I will play golf.

THE JAPANESE VERB*

By now you have probably noticed several things about Japanese verbs. One, of course, is that they come at the very end of the sentence. Japanese is often called a "verb-final language" for that reason. And, since -**masu** forms are always polite, you may have already guessed that each Japanese verb has a more informal form. The informal forms of the verbs you have learned so far are:

Informal (dictionary form)		Polite present- habitual/future (-masu form)	
iku	行く	ikimasu	行きます
kau	買う	kaimasu	買います
miru	見る	mimasu	見ます
nomu	飲む	nomimasu	飲みます
suru	する	shimasu	します
taberu	食べる	tabemasu	食べます
yasumu	休む	yasumimasu	休みます

Other verbs that will be used in this section for demonstration purposes are:

speak	hanasu	話す	hanashimasu	話します
return (home)	kaeru	帰る	kaerimasu	帰ります
come	kuru	来る	kimasu	来ます
hurry	isogu	急ぐ	isogimasu	急ぎます
wait	matsu	待つ	machimasu	待ちます
die	shinu	死ぬ	shinimasu	死にます
call	yobu	呼ぶ	yobimasu	呼びます
get off	oriru	下りる	orimasu	下ります
enter	hairu	入る	hairimasu	入ります

The informal form of the verb is the form normally given in dictionaries, indexes, and most teaching materials (hence its name, the "dictionary form"). Although you have been cautioned about using informal language in your own speech, at this point in your learning you should be aware of these informal verb forms. For one thing, you will often hear them spoken by others. Also, an awareness of them now will help you should you wish to continue your study of Japanese after you finish this book. But perhaps the most important reason is that many new and

---

* Do not feel that you have to memorize everything contained in this section at this time. Read through it for general understanding, and return to it for further study after completing this book.

useful verbs that you learn while in Japan will be presented to you in this informal, dictionary form. Before you can use these verbs yourself, you need to know how to fit them into the polite patterns you have studied in this book.

In other words, you have to know how to form the verb-infinitive (what comes before **-masu**, **-tai desu**, and **-mashō**) from the dictionary form. This will be different depending on the kind of verb involved, for there are three different kinds of verbs in Japanese:

(1) the vowel verb
(2) the consonant verb
(3) the irregular verb

1. THE VOWEL VERB

This type of verb gets its name from the fact that the verb-stem ends in a vowel. The verb-stem is used to build a number of important verb forms. Among them is the verb-infinitive.

(a) Vowel verbs end in **e** + **ru**, or **i** + **ru**
(b) The verb-stem and verb-infinitive are identical: drop the final **ru** of the dictionary form. Look at the examples below.

ending	dict. form	verb-stem	verb-inf.	-masu **form**
-eru	taberu	tabe-	tabe-	tabemasu
-iru	miru	mi-	mi-	mimasu

2. THE CONSONANT VERB

This type of verb gets its name from the fact that the verb-stem ends in a consonant.

(a) Consonant verbs end in **-ku**, **-gu**, **-bu**, **-mu**, **-nu**; a vowel + **ru**; a vowel + **u**; **-su**; or **-tsu**
(b) For consonant verbs ending in **-ku**, **-gu**, **-bu**, **-mu**, **-nu**, a vowel + **ru**, and a vowel + **u**:
verb-stem: drop the final **u**
verb-infinitive: add **i** to the verb-stem

ending	dict. form	verb-stem	verb-inf.	-masu **form**
-ku	iku	ik-	iki-	ikimasu
-gu	isogu	isog-	isogi-	isogimasu
-bu	yobu	yob-	yobi-	yobimasu

-mu	nomu	nom-	nomi-	nomimasu
-nu	shinu	shin-	shini-	shinimasu
vowel+ru	kaeru	kaer-	kaeri-	kaerimasu
vowel+u	kau	ka(w)-	ka(w)i-	kaimasu

Note that the w disappears in **kaimasu**, but appears in certain conjugations not presented in this book. Historically, **w** did exist in Japanese, and for that reason **kau** and other verbs ending in a vowel + **u** are classified as consonant verbs.

(c) For consonant verbs ending in -**su**:
verb-stem: drop the final **u**
verb-infinitive: change the final **s** on the verb-stem to **shi**

| -su | hanasu | hanas- | hanashi- | hanashimasu |

(d) For consonant verbs ending in -**tsu**:
verb-stem: drop the final **su**
verb-infinitive: change the final **t** on the verb-stem to **chi**

| -tsu | matsu | mat- | machi- | machimasu |

Consonant verbs ending in a vowel + **ru** where this vowel is **e** or **i** can often be mistaken for vowel verbs. Simply by looking at their dictionary forms, there is no way of knowing. You can tell quite easily, though, by looking at the verb-stem or the -**masu** form. Compare these examples.

dict. form	verb-stem	verb-inf.	-masu form
oriru	ori-	ori-	orimasu
hairu	hair-	hairi-	hairimasu

Oriru is a vowel verb. **Hairu** is a consonant verb.

3. THE IRREGULAR VERB

There are only two irregular verbs in Japanese. One is **suru**, "to do," and the other is **kuru**, "to come." The verb-stems of both these verbs are quite irregular and vary according to usage. Their verb-infinitives do not change, however.

dict. form	verb-inf.	-masu form
suru	shi-	shimasu
kuru	ki-	kimasu

Chapter 8
(Lessons 31 – 34)

Sentence Patterns Covered in Chapter 8	
Sentence Pattern 28	KIND OF FRUIT + **o** / + NUMBER / + **kudasai.** KIND OF FRUIT + を + NUMBER + く だ さ い 。
Sentence Pattern 29	PLACE + **ni** / + PERSONS + **ga** / **nannin imasu ka?** PLACE + に + PERSONS + が何人いますか? (PLACE + **ni**) / (PERSONS **ga**) / + NUMBER + -**ri** (-**nin**) **imasu.** (PLACE + に) + (PERSONS が) + NUMBER + - り (-人) い ま す 。

In addition to the numbers you studied in Chapter 6, there is another set of numbers that Japanese people use to count items of irregular shape such as candy, fruit, and vegetables, and also to count age up to ten years. These numbers can combine, too, with various counters to show how many bunches, how many boxes, or how many days. With these number words plus the ones in Chapter 6, you should be able to shop or select anything with confidence anywhere in Japan.

Dialogue
店員：いらっしゃい！
お客：この大根はいくらですか？
店員：一本100円です。
お客：あの玉ねぎはいくらですか？

店員　：二つで50円です。
お客　：それは安いですね。
店員　：そうですね。
お客　：じゃあ、大根を二本と玉ねぎを二つください。

お客　：この店は朝何時に開きますか？
店員　：午前六時です。
お客　：早いですね。ここに店員は何人いますか？
店員　：店員は二人います。
お客　：夜いつまでいますか？
店員　：午後八時までです。
お客　：大変ですね。

Clerk	:	Irasshai!	Welcome!
Customer	:	Kono daikon wa ikura desu ka?	How much is this radish?
Clerk	:	Ippon hyaku-en desu.	It's 100 yen for one.
Customer	:	Ano tamanegi wa ikura desu ka?	How much are those onions?
Clerk	:	Futatsu de gojū-en desu.	They're two for 50 yen.
Customer	:	Sore wa yasui desu ne.	They're cheap, aren't they?
Clerk	:	Sō desu ne.	They are, aren't they?
Customer	:	Jā, daikon o ni-hon to tamanegi o futatsu kudasai.	Well then, give me two radishes and two onions.
Customer	:	Kono mise wa asa nanji ni akimasu ka?	What time does this shop open in the morning?
Clerk	:	Gozen roku-ji desu.	At 6 A.M.
Customer	:	Hayai desu ne. Koko ni ten'in wa nannin imasu ka?	That's early isn't it? How many clerks are (work) here?
Clerk	:	Ten'in wa futari imasu.	There are two clerks.
Customer	:	Yoru itsu made imasu ka?	Until when are you here in the evening?
Clerk	:	Gogo hachi-ji made desu.	Until 8 P.M.
Customer	:	Taihen desu ne.	That's tough, isn't it?

Dialogue vocabulary

akimasu	開きます	to open
daikon	大根	a long, white radish
futatsu	二つ	two
gogo	午後	P.M.
gozen	午前	A.M.
ippon	一本	one long, thin object
Itsu?	いつ？	When?
imasu	います	to exist (used for living things)
Nannin?	何人？	How many people?
nippon	二本	two long, thin objects
taihen	大変	difficult, tough
tamanegi	玉ねぎ	onion
ten'in	店員	store clerk
yoru	夜	evening, night

Buying Fruit

In this lesson you will learn a counter that can be used for many types of objects. You will also learn the Japanese words for many types of fruit.

Vocabulary

Numbers

hitotsu	一つ	1 (unit)
futatsu	二つ	2 (units)
mittsu	三つ	3
yottsu	四つ	4
itsutsu	五つ	5
muttsu	六つ	6
nanatsu	七つ	7
yattsu	八つ	8
kokonotsu	九つ	9
tō	十	10
hanbun	半分	one-half
Ikutsu?	いくつ？	How many (units)?

Fruits

kudamono	果物	fruit
kudamonoya	果物屋	fruit shop
banana	バナナ	banana
biwa	びわ	loquat
budō	ぶうど	grape
ichigo	苺	strawberry
kaki	柿	persimmon
mikan	みかん	tangerine
momo	桃	peach
nashi	梨	pear
orenji	オレンジ	orange
ringo	りんご	apple

| sakuranbo | 桜んぼ | cherries |
| suika | 西瓜 | watermelon |

Culture and vocabulary notes

The numbers in the list above can only be used for counting units of ten or less. Since their common suffix -**tsu** (not used in **tō**, "ten") is itself like a counter, the numbers in the form shown above always appear by themselves. In an abbreviated form they are sometimes used with other counters; a few examples of this will be given a bit later in this chapter.

The **de** in **futatsu de** in the dialogue means "for" in that idiomatic expression. Other examples include:

| **mittsu de hyaku-en** | 三つで100円 | three for 100 yen |
| **tō de sen-en** | 十で1,000円 | ten for 1,000 yen |

Remember that the suffix -**ya** in **kudamonoya** indicates a stand or shop. A list of the various types of stores in Japan appears in Appendix 1.

Grammar

Sentence Pattern 28 below is almost identical to the one you learned in Chapter 6:

Hagaki o go-mai kudasai.	Please give me five postcards.
はがきを五枚ください。	
Mikan o itsutsu kudasai.	Please give me five tangerines.
みかんを五つください。	

The word **hanbun**, for "half," is used just like a number in this pattern.

Sentence Pattern 28	
KIND OF FRUIT + **o** / + NUMBER / + **kudasai.**	Please give me + NUMBER +
KIND OF FRUIT + を + NUMBER + ください。	KIND OF FRUIT.

Examples

Ringo o hitotsu kudasai.	Please give me one apple.
リンゴを一つください。	
Mikan o itsutsu kudasai.	Please give me five tangerines.
みかんを五つください。	

Momo o mittsu kudasai.　　　　　　Please give me three peaches.
桃を三つください。

Suika o hanbun kudasai.　　　　　　Please give me half a watermelon.
西瓜を半分ください。

Practice

1. Practice saying the following sentences aloud.

Ringo o hitotsu kudasai.　　　　　　Please give me one apple.
リンゴを一つください。

Mikan o futatsu kudasai.　　　　　　Please give me two tangerines.
みかんを二つください。

Nashi o yottsu kudasai.　　　　　　Please give me four pears.
梨を四つください。

Kaki o itsutsu kudasai.　　　　　　Please give me five persimmons.
柿を五つください。

Suika o futatsu kudasai.　　　　　　Please give me two watermelons.
西瓜を二つください。

Suika o hanbun kudasai.　　　　　　Please give me half a watermelon.
西瓜を半分ください。

2. What do you say when you want to buy these items at a fruit stand? Turn to page 239 for the answers.
   (a) Three persimmons
   (b) Ten tangerines
   (c) Six peaches
   (d) Four pears
   (e) Seven oranges
   (f) Eight apples
   (g) half a watermelon

• LESSON 32 •

Buying Vegetables

In this lesson you will learn how to purchase vegetables and also the Japanese words for many vegetables.

Vocabulary

yaoya	やお屋	vegetable stand
yasai	野菜	vegetable(s)
o-kyaku	お客	customer
shujin	主人	shop owner
ingen	いんげん	string bean
jagaimo	じゃがいも	potato
karifurawā	カリフラワー	cauliflower
kyabetsu	キャベツ	cabbage
nasu	なす	eggplant
negi (naganegi)	ねぎ（長ねぎ）	green onion, scallion
piiman	ピーマン	green pepper
retasu	レタス	lettuce
tamanegi	玉ねぎ	onion
tomato	トマト	tomato

Grammar

Different words and phrases may be used to purchase vegetables, depending on how they are packed and their shapes. Several examples are shown below.

1. Buying as many as you need

Vegetables are often packed loose in boxes at small vegetable shops, so you only have to buy as many as you need. For loosely packed vegetables, use the same sentence pattern that you did for buying fruit in Lesson 31.

2. Buying Bunches and Boxes

Vegetables and fruit can also be piled on plates, tied in bunches, or packed in boxes for convenience. An abbreviated form of the numbers in the **hitotsu** series plus an appropriate counter is used to ask for vegetables that are displayed like this.

hito-	一一	1	itsu-	五一	5	ya-	八一	8
futa-	二一	2	mu-	六一	6	kyū-	九一	9
mi-	三一	3	nana-	七一	7	tō-	十一	10
yo-	四一	4						

You will note that **kyū**- is used here instead of **kokono**-. Three counters used with these forms are:

-fusa	一房	bunch
-yama	一山	pile (literally, mountain)
-hako	一箱	box

These can be used as independent words as well. When used as counters they are used in much the same way as the counter -**mai**.

Budō o mifusa kudasai.
ぶどうを三房ください。
Please give me three bunches of grapes.

Ichigo o futahako kudasai.
苺を二箱ください。
Please give me two boxes of strawberries.

Tamanegi o hitoyama kudasai.
玉ねぎを一山ください。
Please give me one pile of onions.

Tomato o miyama kudasai.
トマトを三山ください。
Please give me three piles of tomatoes.

3. Buying Long and Thin Vegetables

If the vegetable is one that is long and thin, the counter -**hon** is used with the numbers of the **ichi** series that you learned in Chapter 6. Note the sound changes that occur.

ippon	一本	1
ni-hon	二本	2
san-bon	三本	3
yon-hon	四本	4
go-hon	五本	5
roppon	六本	6
shichi-hon (nana-hon)	七本	7

hachi-hon (happon)	八本	8
kyū-hon	九本	9
juppon (jippon)	十本	10

Examples of vegetables that may be used with this counter are:

daikon	大根	long white radish
gobō	ごぼう	burdock (root)
kyūri	きゅうり	cucumber
ninjin	にんじん	carrot

The counter -**hon** may also be used with objects like pens, pencils, bottles, and umbrellas—anything that is long and thin.

Practice

1. Practice saying the following sentences aloud.

Jagaimo o mittsu to retasu o hitotsu kudasai.
じゃがいもを三つとレタスを一つください。

Please give me three potatoes and one head of lettuce.

Tamanegi o yottsu to kyabetsu o futatsu kudasai.
玉ねぎを四つとキャベツを二つください。

Please give me four onions and two cabbages.

Nasu o yattsu to karifurawā o hitotsu kudasai.
なすを八つとカリフラワーを一つください。

Please give me eight eggplants and one cauliflower.

Retasu o futatsu to jagaimo o kokonotsu kudasai.
レタスを二つとじゃがいもを九つください。

Please give me two heads of lettuce and nine potatoes.

Piiman o itsutsu to tomato o muttsu kudasai.
ピーマンを五つとトマトを六つください。

Please give me five green peppers and six tomatoes.

2. What do you say when you want to buy these items at a vegetable stand? Turn to page 239 for the answers.
   (a) Six potatoes
   (b) Two cabbages
   (c) Five eggplants
   (d) Three heads of lettuce
   (e) One cauliflower
   (f) Seven onions
   (g) Five tomatoes

3. Practice saying the following sentences aloud.

   Sakuranbo o hitohako kudasai.   Please give me one box of cherries.
   桜んぼを一箱ください。

   Biwa o hitoyama kudasai.   Please give me one pile of loquats.
   びわを一山ください。

   Banana o hitofusa kudasai.   Please give me one bunch of bananas.
   バナナを一房ください。

   Tomato o miyama kudasai.   Please give me three piles of tomatoes.
   トマトを三山ください。

4. Express thes following in Japanese. Turn to page 239 for the answers.
   (a) One bunch of bananas
   (b) One box of strawberries
   (c) One pile of onions
   (d) One pile of tomatoes
   (e) One box of cherries
   (f) Two bunches of grapes
   (g) One pile of persimmons
   (h) One pile of tangerines

Counting People

In this lesson you will learn how to ask and respond to the question *How many people are there?* You will also learn the counter for the number of people.

Vocabulary

hitori	一人	1 person
futari	二人	2 persons
san-nin	三人	3 persons
yo-nin	四人	4 persons
go-nin	五人	5 persons
roku-nin	六人	6 persons
nana-nin (shichi-nin)	七人	7 persons
hachi-nin	八人	8 persons
kyū-nin	九人	9 persons
jū-nin	十人	10 persons
Nannin?	何人？	How many persons?
iru/imasu	います	to exist (usually for humans and animals)
ryokan	旅館	Japanese-style inn

Culture and vocabulary notes

When counting people, abbreviated forms from the **hitotsu** series are used with the counter -*ri* for one or two people. For three or more, numbers from the **ichi** series with the counter -**nin** are used.

The verb **imasu** means "to exist" or "to be present" and is generally used only for animate beings (humans or animals).

Grammar

Sentence Pattern 29	
PLACE + **ni** / + PERSONS + **ga** / **nannin imasu ka?** PLACE + に + PERSONS + が + 何人いますか？	How many + PERSONS + are there in + PLACE?
(PLACE + **ni**) / + (PERSONS + **ga**) / + NUMBER + -**ri** (-**nin**) **imasu.** (PLACE + に) + (PERSONS + が) + -人います。	There are + NUMBER + (persons) + (in place).

Examples

Koko ni sensei ga nannin imasu ka? ここに先生が何人いますか？
How many teachers are here?

(Koko ni) sensei ga futari imasu. （ここに）先生が二人います。
There are two teachers here.

Ryokan ni Amerika-jin ga nannin imasu ka? 旅館にアメリカ人が何人いますか？
How many Americans are there in the inn?

When combined with the verb **imasu**, **ni** indicates where the subject of **imasu** exists. **Ga** indicates the subject, who it is that exists. In this sense, **ga** is different from **wa**, which shows who or what is being talked about.

The person-counter can also be used in the following way:

Tōkyō e nannin ikimasu ka? 東京へ何人いきますか？
How many people are going to Tokyo?

Sensei ga futari to gakusei ga roku-nin ikimasu. 先生が二人と学生が六人行きます。
Two teachers and six students are going.

Practice

Express the following in Japanese. Turn to page 239 to check your answers.

1. There are two children.
2. There are three adults.
3. There will be five students.
4. There are four teachers.
5. There were six Americans.
6. Are there eight Japanese?

Keeping Track of the Time

In this lesson you will learn various expressions and words related to time, including the names of the days of the month, days of the week, months, and seasons. You will also learn how to ask when something will take place, how long it will last, and when it will be over.

Vocabulary

tsuitachi	一日	1st day (but pronounced **ichinichi** to mean "one day")
futsuka	二日	2nd day; 2 days
mikka	三日	3rd day; 3 days
yokka	四日	4th day; 4 days
itsuka	五日	5th day; 5 days
muika	六日	6th day; 6 days
nanoka (nanuka)	七日	7th day; 7 days
yōka	八日	8th day; 8 days
kokonoka	九日	9th day; 9 days
tōka	十日	10th day; 10 days
jūichi-nichi	十一日	11th day; 11 days
jūninichi	十二日	12th day; 12 days
jūsannichi	十三日	13th day; 13 days
jūyokka	十四日	14th day; 14 days
jūgonichi	十五日	15th day; 15 days
jūrokunichi	十六日	16th day; 16 days
jūshichinichi	十七日	17th day; 17 days
jūhachinichi	十八日	18th day; 18 days
jūkunichi	十九日	19th day; 19 days
hatsuka	二十日	20th day; 20 days
nijūichinichi	二十一日	21st day; 21 days
nijūninichi	二十二日	22nd day; 22 days
nijūsannichi	二十三日	23rd day; 23 days
nijūyokka	二十四日	24th day; 24 days

nijūgonichi	二十五日	25th day; 25 days
nijūrokunichi	二十六日	26th day; 26 days
nijūshichinichi (nijūnananichi)	二十七日	27th day; 27 days
nijūhachinichi	二十八日	28th day; 28 days
nijūkunichi	二十九日	29th day; 29 days
sanjū-nichi	三十日	30th day; 30 days
sanjūichinichi	三十一日	31st day; 31 days
Nannichi?	何日？	What day? How many days?
au/aimasu	会う/ 会います	to meet
benkyō o suru/shimasu	勉強をする/ します	to study
gurai (kurai)	ぐらい/くらい	about, approximately
Itsu?	いつ？	When?
gozen	午前	A.M., in the morning
gogo	午後	P.M., in the afternoon
kakaru/kakarimasu	かかる/ かかります	to require, take, involve
mainichi	毎日	everyday

Culture and vocabulary notes

You will notice that slightly variant forms of the numbers in the **hitotsu** series are used for the first to the tenth days and for one to ten days (except for one day, which has a special form). After that, the numbers in the **ichi** series plus the counter -**nichi** are used (except for the twentieth day, **hatsuka***)*.

Grammar
1. Finding out "When"

In Chapter 6 you learned these sentences.

Nanji ni Kyōto e ikimashō ka?　　At what time shall we go to Kyoto?
何時に京都へ行きましょうか？

San-ji ni ikimashō.　　Let's go at 3:00.
三時に行きましょう？

Using **itsu**, "when," or **nannichi ni**, "on what day," you can construct sentences like these.

Itsu Kyōto e ikimasu ka? いつ京都へ行きますか？	When are you going Kyoto?
Nannichi ni Kyōto e ikimasu ka? 何日に京都へ行きますか？	What day are you going to Kyoto?
Itsu aimashō ka? いつ会いましょうか？	When shall we meet?
Jūyokka ni aimashō. 十四日に会いましょう。	Let's meet on the 14th.
Nannichi ni aimashō ka? 何日に会いましょうか？	On what day shall we meet?
Tōka ni aimashō. 十日に会いましょう。	Let's meet on the 10th.
Itsu Amerika e ikimasu ka? いつアメリカへ行きますか？	When are you going America?
Tōka no gogo ni-ji ni ikimasu. 十日の午後二時に行きます。	I'm going at 2:00 in the afternoon on the 10th.

The particle **ni** is used here to specify a point in time. It is also used with the question word **nannichi** but not with **itsu**.

Study the word order that is used in the last example above: **tōka no gogo niji ni** (first the day, then the part of the day, then the hour). Consecutively smaller, more precise time designations are used in Japanese, while English does just the opposite (compare the Japanese with the English translation). Think of the particle **no** in this phrase as indicating "the afternoon *of the* 10th day."

2. Finding out "How long"

The days of the month can also be used to express duration of time. For example, **tōka** can mean either "the tenth day of the month" or it can mean "a period of ten days." The words you learned in Chapter 6 for expressing the hour, however, can only mean the specific time of day. The counter **-kan** is used with these words to express duration of time in hours.

ichi-jikan	一時間	1 hour
ni-jikan	二時間	2 hours

san-jikan	三時間	3 hours
*yo-jikan	四時間	4 hours
go-jikan	五時間	5 hours
roku-jikan	六時間	6 hours
shichi-jikan (nana-jikan)	七時間	7 hours
hachi-jikan	八時間	8 hours
ku-jikan	九時間	9 hours
jū-jikan	十時間	10 hours
jūichi-jikan	十一時間	11 hours
jūni-jikan	十二時間	12 hours

To ask how many days or hours something will take, use the word **gurai (kurai)**, "about" or "approximately," and a form of the verb **kakaru / kakarimasu**. (**Kakaru** has many meanings; among them are "require," "involve," and "take.")

Nanjikan gurai kakarimasu ka? About how many hours will it take?
何時間ぐらいかかりますか？

Ni-jikan gurai kakarimasu. It will take about two hours.
二時間ぐらいかかります。

Nannichi gurai kakarimasu ka? About how many days will it take?
何日ぐらいかかりますか？

Tōka gurai kakarimasu. It will take about ten days.
十日ぐらいかかります。

Gurai (kurai) can also be used with other verbs. For example:

Nannichi gurai Nihon ni imasu ka? About how many days will
何日ぐらい日本にいますか？ you be in Japan?

Kyō nanjikan gurai tenisu o shimasu ka? About how many hours will
今日何時間ぐらいテニスをしますか？ you play tennis today?

Ni is not used above because these sentences do not refer to specific points in time.

3. Finding out "Until when"

If you want to know until when something will happen, you can ask the following:

Nannichi made Nihon ni imasu ka?   Until what day will you be in Japan?
何日まで日本にいますか？

Itsu made Nihon ni imasu ka?   Until when will you be in Japan?
いつまで日本にいますか？

Made was briefly introduced in Chapter 6, where it was used to mean "to," "up to," or "far as." For example, **Tōkyō Eki made ikura desu ka?** means "How much does it cost to go as far as Tokyo station?" **Made** always fixes a limit. For example, compare:

Nihon e ikimasu.   I'm going to Japan.
日本へ行きます。
(**e** denotes general direction)

Nihon made ikimasu.   I'm going as far as Japan.
日本まで行きます。
(but no farther; **made** here denotes a specific or final destination)

Thus, in answer to the question, **Nannichi (itsu) made Nihon ni imasu ka?** your response, **Jūgonichi made imasu**, means simply that you intend to stay until the 15th of the month but not beyond. Some more examples.

ku-ji made	九時まで	until 9:00
ashita made	明日まで	until tomorrow
konban made	今晩まで	until this evening

4. Naming the Days, Months, and Seasons

Vocabulary

Days of the Week

Nichiyōbi	日曜日	Sunday
Getsuyōbi	月曜日	Monday
Kayōbi	火曜日	Tuesday
Suiyōbi	水曜日	Wednesday
Mokuyōbi	木曜日	Thursday

Kin-yōbi	金曜日	Friday
Doyōbi	土曜日	Saturday
Nan-yōbi?	何曜日？	What day of the week?

Months

Ichigatsu	一月	January
Nigatsu	二月	February
Sangatsu	三月	March
Shigatsu	四月	April
Gogatsu	五月	May
Rokugatsu	六月	June
Shichigatsu	七月	July
Hachigatsu	八月	August
Kugatsu	九月	September
Jūgatsu	十月	October
Jūichigatsu	十一月	November
Junigatsu	十二月	December
Nangatsu?	何月？	What month?

Seasons

haru	春	spring
natsu	夏	summer
aki	秋	autumn, fall
fuyu	冬	winter

Culture and vocabulary notes

Recall that the words for this month, last month, and next month (**kongetsu, sengetsu, raigetsu**) end with -**getsu**. The names of the months end with -*gatsu*, which is slightly different. Try not to confuse them.

Such words as **kyō**, **kinō**, **kotoshi**, **kyonen**, and **rainen** do not *require* the particle **ni**. To say "on Sunday," "at 8 o'clock," "in January," and the like, however, the particle **ni** is used, as in **Nichiyōbi ni**, **hachi-ji ni**, and **Ichigatsu ni**.

Practice

1. Practice saying the following dialogues aloud.

Itsu aimashō ka? いつ会いましょうか？	When shall we meet?
Yokka no jū-ji ni aimashō. 四日の十時に会いましょう。	Let's meet at 10:00 on the 4th.
Itsu ikimashō ka? いつ行きましょうか？	When shall we go?
Mikka no gozen jū-ji ni ikimashō. 三日の午前十時に行きましょう。	Let's go at 10:00 on the morning of the 3rd.
Kokonoka ni ikimasu ka? 九日に行きますか？	Are you going on the 9th?
Iie, tōka ni ikimasu. いいえ、十日に行きます。	No, I'm going on the 10th.
Densha de Kyōto e ikimasu. 電車で京都へ行きます。	I'm going to Kyoto by train.
Nanjikan gurai kakarimasu ka? 何時間ぐらいかかりますか？	About how many hours will it take?
Gojikan gurai kakarimasu. 五時間ぐらいかかります。	It will take about five hours.
Nannichi gurai Amerika ni imasu ka? 何日ぐらいアメリカにいますか？	About how many days will you be in America?
Futsuka gurai imasu. 二日ぐらいいます。	About two days.
Mainichi nanjikan gurai benkyō o shi-masu ka? 毎日何時間ぐらい勉強をしますか？	About how many hours a day do you study?
Mainichi san-jikan gurai benkyō o shimasu. 毎日三時間ぐらい勉強をします。	I study about three hours every day.
Densha de nanjikan gurai kakarimashita ka? 電車で何時間ぐらいかかりましたか？	About how many hours did it take by train?

San-jikan gurai kakarimashita.
三時間ぐらいかかりました。

It took about three hours.

Nannichi gurai Kyōto ni imashita ka?
何日ぐらい京都にいましたか？

About how many days were you in Kyoto?

Muika gurai imashita.
六日ぐらいいました。

I was there about six days.

Nannichi made Nihon ni imasu ka?
何日まで日本にいますか？

Until what day will you be in Japan?

Hatsuka made imasu.
二十日まています。

Until the 20th.

Nanji made benkyō o shimasu ka?
何時まで勉強をしますか？

Until what time will you study?

Jū-ji made benkyō o shimasu.
十時まで勉強をします。

I'll study until 10:00.

Itsu made Furansu ni imashita ka?
いつまでフランスにいましたか？

Until when were you in France?

Hatsuka made imashita.
二十日までいました。

Until the 20th.

Itsu made tenisu o shimasu ka?
いつまでテニスをしますか？

Until when will you play tennis?

Go-ji made tenisu o shimasu.
五時までテニスをします。

I'll play tennis until 5:00.

2. Practice the seasons and months by repeating the following sentences aloud.

Nihon no haru wa Sangatsu to Shigatsu to Gogatsu desu.
日本の春は三月と四月と五月です。

Japanese spring is March, April, and May.

Nihon no natsu wa Rokugatsu to Shichigatsu to Hachigatsu desu.
日本の夏は六月と七月と八月です。

Japanese summer is June, July, and August.

Nihon no aki wa Kugatsu to Jūgatsu to Jūichigatsu desu.
日本の秋は九月と十月と十一月です。

Japanese autumn is September, October, and November.

Nihon no fuyu wa Jūnigatsu to Ichigatsu to
  Nigatsu desu.
日本の冬は十二月と一月と二月です。

Japanese winter is
  December, January,
  and February.

3. Practice repeating the following dialogue aloud.

Ima nangatsu desu ka?
今何月ですか？

What month is it now?

Rokugatsu desu.
六月です。

It's June.

Nangatsu ni Nihon e ikimasu ka?
何月に日本へ行きますか？

What month are you going to
  Japan?

Ichigatsu tōka ni ikimasu.
一月十日に行きます。

I'm going on the 10th of January.

Itsu Amerika e ikimasu ka?
いつアメリカへ行きますか？

When are you going to America?

Rainen Amerika e ikimasu.
来年アメリカへ行きます。

I'm going to America next year.

Kyō wa nan-yōbi desu ka?
今日何曜日ですか？

What day is it today?

Getsuyobi desu.
月曜日です。

It's Monday.

Chapter 9
(Lessons 35 – 42)

Sentence Patterns Covered in Chapter 9	
Sentence Pattern 30	Dōzo / + VERB + -te FORM + kudasai. どうぞ + VERB + -て form + ください。
Sentence Pattern 30A	(Kono) + COLOR + (no) + NOUN + o / misete kudasai. (この) + COLOR + (の) + NOUN + を見せて ください。
Sentence Pattern 30B	PLACE NAME + e / itte kudasai. PLACE NAME + へ行ってください。 PLACE NAME + made / o-negai shimasu. PLACE NAME + までおねがいします。
Sentence Pattern 30C	Dokoka / + KIND OF PLACE + o / oshiete kudasai. どこか + KIND OF PLACE + を教えて ください。
Sentence Pattern 31	COLOR + NOUN + ga / arimasu ka? COLOR + NOUN + がありますか？
Sentence Pattern 32	NOUN + ga / wakarimasu ka? NOUN + が分かりますか？

Japanese politeness and hospitality are renowned the world over. And Japanese people often look for these qualities in others. Demonstrating good manners in your speech will make your stay in Japan more pleasant for you and your hosts.

In this chapter you will learn how to produce "request" sentences or "polite imperative" sentences in Japanese. In English, requests can be made in many different ways: "Come in," "Please come in," "Do come in," "Will you come in?" "Won't you come in?"

One way to make a request in Japanese is to use what is called the *"-te* form" of the verb plus the word **kudasai**, "please." A detailed explanation of how to form the -**te** form appears at the end of this chapter. For now, study the -**te** forms of various verbs as they are used in Lesson 35.

Dialogue

タクシーで：

リサ　　　　　　　：どこかいいデパートを教えてください。
タクシードライバー：ええ、分かりました。十分ぐらいかかり
　　　　　　　　　　ます。
リサ　　　　　　　：そこまで行ってください。

デパートで：

店員：いらっしゃいませ！何を差し上げましょうか？
リサ：英語が分かりますか？
店員：いいえ、すみません。日本語を話してください。
リサ：携帯電話はありますか？
店員：はい、どうぞ見てください。
リサ：あの黄色い携帯を見せてください。
店員：はい、どうぞ。
リサ：これはいくらですか？
店員：13,000円です。
リサ：もう少し安い携帯がありますか？
店員：これはいかがですか？10,000円です。
リサ：はい、これをください。
店員：それから、何か他にありますか？
リサ：MP-3プレイヤーはありますか？
店員：はい、あります。これはどうですか？8,000円です。

リサ　：いいですね。じゃあ、それだけです。
店員　：はい、分かりました。18,000円いただきます。
リサ　：お願いします。
店員　：20,000円お預かりします。2,000円のおつりです。
リサ　：ありがとう。
店員　：ありがとうございました！

In a taxi:

Lisa	: **Dokoka ii depāto o oshiete kudasai.**	Please tell me of a good department store somewhere.
Taxi driver	: **Ē, wakarimashita. Jū-pun gurai kakarimasu.**	Okay, I understand. It will take about ten minutes.
Lisa	: **Soko made itte kudasai.**	Please go there.

At a department store:

Clerk	: **Irasshaimase! Nani o sashiagemashō ka?**	Welcome! What shall (can) I do for you?
Lisa	: **Eigo ga wakarimasu ka?**	Do you understand English?
Clerk	: **Iie, sumimasen. Nihongo o hanashite kudasai.**	No, sorry I don't. Please speak Japanese.
Lisa	: **Keitai denwa wa arimasu ka?**	Do you have cell phones?
Clerk	: **Hai, dōzo mite kudasai.**	Yes, please take a look.
Lisa	: **Ano kiiroi keitai o misete kudasai.**	Please show me that yellow cell phone.
Clerk	: **Hai, dōzo.**	Here you are.
Lisa	: **Kore wa ikura desu ka?**	How much is this?
Clerk	: **Ichiman-sanzen-en desu.**	It's ¥13,000.
Lisa	: **Mō sukoshi yasui keitai ga arimasu ka?**	Do you have a little less expensive one?
Clerk	: **Kore wa ikaga desu ka? Ichiman-en desu.**	How about this? It's ¥10,000.
Lisa	: **Hai. Kore o kudasai.**	Yes. I'll take this.
Clerk	: **Sore kara, nanika hoka ni arimasu ka?**	Is there anything else that I can help you with?
Lisa	: **MP-3 pureiyā wa arimasu ka?**	Do you have MP-3 players?

Clerk :	Hai, arimasu. Kore wa dō desu ka? Hassen-en desu.	Yes, we have some. How about this one? It's ¥8,000.
Lisa :	Ii desu ne. Jā, sore dake desu.	That's good. Okay, that's all (that I need).
Clerk :	Hai, wakarimashita. Ichiman hassen-en itadakimasu.	I understand. That will be ¥18,000.
Lisa :	Onegai shimasu.	Please (help me).
Clerk :	Niman-en o azukari shimasu. Nisen-en no o-tsuri desu.	That's ¥20,000. Your change is ¥2,000.
Lisa:	Arigatō.	Thank you.
Clerk:	Arigatō gozaimashita!	Thank you very much!

Dialogue vocabulary

arimasu	あります	to exist (usually for inanimate things); to have
azukari shimasu	預かりします	to keep; take care of
dokoka	どこか	somewhere
Dō desu ka?	どうですか？	How?; How about?
hoka ni	他に	other; else
Ikura desu ka?	いくらですか？	How much does it cost?
keitai denwa / keitai	携帯電話/携帯	cellphone
kiiroi	黄色い	yellow
mō sukoshi	もう少し	a little more
MP-3 pureiyā	MP-3プレイヤー	MP-3 player
nanika	何か	something
o-tsuri	おつり	change (money)
sashiageru	差し上げる	to give; to offer (polite)
sumimasen	すみません	sorry

Culture and vocabulary notes

Sashiageru is an extremely polite form of the verb ageru and is often used by clerks or shopkeepers to customers. Another use of dōzo in an offering situation is shown in Hai, dōzo. The expression Mō sukoshi means "a little bit more."

Making Requests and Offers

In this lesson you will learn a new verb-form that can be used to offer someone something or to make a request.

Vocabulary

agaru / agarimasu	上がる/上がります	to go up; to climb
dōzo	どうぞ	Please (take this).
iu / iimasu	言う/言います	to say
kaku / kakimasu	書く/書きます	to write
kiru / kimasu	着る/着ます	to wear
yomu / yomimasu	読む/読みます	to read

Culture and vocabulary notes

Dōzo is often used when offering something to another person. In the examples below it makes the request warmer and perhaps more personal than if it were omitted. The expression **Dōzo agatte kudasai** is used when welcoming a guest to one's home. The meaning "Please come up" refers to the fact that when entering a Japanese home, one removes one's shoes at the entrance and literally "steps up" into the house. Alternately, the expression **Dōzo haitte kudasai** "Please enter" may be used.

Grammar

The following sentence pattern provides you with one of the simplest and most commonly used patterns in Japanese. Many of the verbs in the examples are new ones for you. Study them carefully and do your best to memorize them, for they will come in very handy in your daily activities.

Sentence Pattern 30	
Dōzo / + VERB + -**te** FORM + **kudasai.** どうぞ + VERB + -て FORM + ください。	Please + VERB.

Examples

iku / ikimasu	Dōzo itte kudasai. どうぞ行ってください。	Please go.
kau / kaimasu	Dōzo katte kudasai. どうぞ買ってください。	Please buy.
miru / mimasu	Dōzo mite kudasai. どうぞ見てください。	Please look.
nomu / nomimasu	Dōzo nonde kudasai. どうぞ飲んでください。	Please drink.
suru / shimasu	Dōzo shite kudasai. どうぞしてください。	Please do.
taberu / tabemasu	Dōzo tabete kudasai. どうぞ食べてください。	Please eat.
agaru / agarimasu	Dōzo agatte kudasai. どうぞ上がってください。	Please come up.
hairu / hairimasu	Dōzo haitte kudasai. どうぞ入ってください。	Please enter.
hanasu / hanashimasu	Dōzo hanashite kudasai. どうぞ話してください。	Please speak.
isogu / isogimasu	Dōzo isoide kudasai. どうぞ急いでください。	Please hurry.
iu / iimasu	Dōzo itte kudasai. どうぞ言ってください。	Please say.
kaeru / kaerimasu	Dōzo kaette kudasai. どうぞ帰ってください。	Please return.
kaku / kakimasu	Dōzo kaite kudasai. どうぞ書いてください。	Please write.
kiku / kikimasu	Dōzo kiite kudasai. どうぞ聞いてください。	Please listen.
kiru / kimasu	Dōzo kite kudasai. どうぞ着てください。	Please wear.
kuru / kimasu	Dōzo kite kudasai. どうぞ来てください。	Please come.
matsu / machimasu	Dōzo matte kudasai. どうぞ待ってください。	Please wait.
miseru / misemasu	Dōzo misete kudasai. どうぞ見せてください。	Please show.

oshieru / oshiemasu	Dōzo oshiete kudasai. どうぞ教えてください。	Please teach.
yomu / yomimasu	Dōzo yonde kudasai. どうぞ読んでください。	Please read.

The -te form (-de in isoide, nonde, yonde) is most often used with a following word or phrase; in this sentence pattern, the word that follows is kudasai. Note that the -te forms of iku and iu and the -te forms of kuru and kiru sound the same (although they are written differently in Japanese). Context will determine which meaning is intended.

When offering food or drink to someone, the following construction can be used.

Dōzo biiru o nonde kudasai. どうぞビールを飲んでください。	Please have some beer.
Dōzo Hawai no kudamono o tabete kudasai. どうぞハワイの果物を食べてください。	Please have some Hawaiian fruit.

Practice

Practice saying the following sentences aloud. Think of them as offers to someone rather than requests.

Dōzo agatte kudasai. どうぞ上がってください。	Please come up (enter).
Dōzo sono kimono o kite kudasai. どうぞその着物を着てください。	Please wear that kimono.
Dōzo kono hon o yonde kudasai. どうぞこの本を読んでください。	Please read this book.
Dōzo kore o mite kudasai. どうぞこれを見てください。	Please look at this.
Dōzo Nihongo o hanashite kudasai. どうぞ日本語を話してください。	Please speak Japanese.
Dōzo orenji jusu o nonde kudasai. どうぞオレンジジュスを飲んでください。	Please have some orange juice.
Dōzo kiite kudasai. どうぞ聞いてください。	Please listen.

Requesting Things at a Department Store

In this lesson you learn how to ask whether a certain item is available at a store and how to request that the store clerk show it to you. In addition, you will learn the Japanese words for various colors.

Vocabulary
Adjectives

akai	赤い	red
aoi	青い	blue
chairoi	茶色い	brown
kiiroi	黄色い	yellow
kuroi	黒い	black
shiroi	白い	white

Borrowed Nouns

beiju	ベイジュ	beige color
gurei	グレイ	gray color
guriin	グリーン	green color
orenji	オレンジ	orange color
pinku	ピンク	pink color
rabendā	ラベンダー	lavender color

Other Vocabulary

aru/arimasu	ある/あります	to exist (usually for inanimate things)
chikatetsu	地下鉄	subway
midori	緑	green
murasaki	紫	purple

Culture and vocabulary notes

Note that some color terms come in an adjective form and some in a noun form. The borrowed nouns in the above list are only a few among the many in this category. They are very popular in the cosmetic and fashion worlds of Japan, which have been strongly influenced by the West.

Sentence Pattern 31 introduces one of the most commonly used verbs in one of the most commonly used patterns. You can use it in department stores, restaurants, bookshops, and the like to find out whether the item you want is available or not.

Grammar

Sentence Pattern 31	
COLOR + NOUN + **ga** / **arimasu ka?** COLOR + NOUN + が あ り ま す か？	Do you have (Is there) a + COLOR + NOUN?

Examples

Shiroi sētā ga arimasu ka? 白 い セ ー タ ー が あ り ま す か？	Do you have a white sweater?
Akai sukāfu ga arimasu ka? 赤 い ス カ ー フ が あ り ま す か？	Do you have any red scarves?
Gurei no surakkusu ga arimasu ka? グ レ イ の ス ラ ッ ク ス が あ り ま す か？	Are there any gray slacks (i.e., slacks of gray color)?
Beiju no kōto ga arimasu ka? ベ イ ジ ュ の コ ー ト が あ り ま す か？	Do you have a beige coat?

Notice that adjective color terms can be applied to nouns directly but that noun color terms use the particle **no** before the nouns they modify.

The verb **arimasu** is used in much the same way as **imasu**, except that it is generally used for inanimate things. The particle **ga** shows what it is that exists or is present. The particle **ni** is used to show where the item exists.

Kyōto ni chikatetsu ga arimasu ka? 京 都 に 地 下 鉄 が あ り ま す か？	Is there a subway in Kyoto?

Arimasu can also imply ownership or possession. Thus, in the sentence **Beiju no kōto ga arimasu ka?** you might be asking whether there are beige overcoats in a store or whether a friend happens to own a beige overcoat.

When you've discovered that the item you want is available, ask to see it using the following sentence pattern.

Sentence Pattern 31A	
(Kono) + COLOR + (no) + NOUN + o / misete kudasai. (この) + COLOR + (の) + NOUN + を見せてください。	Please show me (this) + COLOR + NOUN.

Example

Akai reinkōto o misete kudasai.
赤いレインコートを見せてください。

Please show me a red raincoat.

Kiiroi sētā o misete kudasai.
黄色いセーターを見せてください。

Please show me a yellow sweater.

Ano kuroi kōto o misete kudasai.
あの黒いコートを見せてください。

Please show me that black coat (over there).

Sono aoi kimono o misete kudasai.
その青いコートを見せてください。

Please show me that blue kimono (near you).

Guriin no reinkōto o misete kudasai.
グリーンのレインコートを見せてください。

Please show me some green raincoats.

Beiju no kōto o misete kudasai.
ベイジュのコートを見せてください。

Please show me some beige coats.

Practice

Practice saying the following sentences aloud.

1. Shiroi sētā ga arimasu ka?
    白いセーターがありますか？

    Do you have a white sweater? (Are there any white sweaters?)

    Kuroi kōto ga arimasu ka?
    黒いコートがありますか？

    Do you have a black coat?

    Akai sukāfu ga arimasu ka?
    赤いスカーフがありますか？

    Do you have a red scarf?

    Kiiroi reinkōto ga arimasu ka?
    黄色いレインコートがありますか？

    Do you have a yellow raincoat?

    Chairoi sūtsu ga arimasu ka?
    茶色いスーツがありますか？

    Do you have a brown suit?

2. **Gurei no surakkusu ga arimasu ka?**
   グレイのスラックスがありますか？

   Pinku no sētā ga arimasu ka?
   ピンクのセーターがありますか？

   Beiju no kōto ga arimasu ka?
   ベイジュのコートがありますか？

   Guriin no reinkōto ga arimasu ka?
   グリンのレインコートがありますか？

Do you have any gray slacks?

Do you have a pink sweater?

Do you have a beige coat?

Do you have a green raincoat?

Giving Directions to a Taxi Driver

In this lesson you will learn how to ask a driver to take you to a certain location.

Vocabulary

hikōjō	飛行場	airport
kūkō	空港	airport
made	まで	as far as
O-negai shimasu.	お願いします。	Please (help me).

Culture and vocabulary notes

O-negai shimasu is a very common phrase used in requests. It can be used instead of **kudasai** in a request like **Biiru o o-negai shimasu.** But it does not follow a verb -*te* form. **Ginza made o-negai shimasu** could be literally translated as "As far as the Ginza, please."

When speaking to a taxi driver, make sure you pronounce the place name very clearly. The best way to avoid misunderstanding is to ask a Japanese friend or hotel clerk to write your destination in Japanese on a piece of paper that you can show to the taxi driver.

Grammar

Sentence Pattern 30B

PLACE NAME + **e / itte kudasai.** PLACE NAME + へ行ってください。 PLACE NAME + **made / o-negai shimasu.** PLACE NAME + までお願いします。	Please go to + PLACE + NAME.

Example

Ginza e itte kudasai.
銀座へ行ってください。

Please go to the Ginza.

Hikōjō made o-negai shimasu.
飛行場までお願いします。

Please go to the airport.

Tōkyō Daigaku e itte kudasai.
東京大学へ行ってください。

Please go to Tokyo University.

Practice

1. Practice asking a taxi driver to take you to the following places in Tokyo.

Ginza 銀座	**Yotsuya** 四谷
Shinjuku Eki 新宿駅	**Roppongi** 六本木
Tōkyō Eki 東京駅	**Shibuya** 渋谷
Narita Kūkō 成田空港	**Ueno Eki** 上野駅

Making Sure You Understand and are Understood

In this lesson you will learn the Japanese words for various languages and also how to ask whether someone understands that language.

VOCABULARY

Chūgokugo	中国語	Chinese language
Doitsugo	ドイツ語	German
Furansugo	フランス語	French
Itariago	イタリア語	Italian
Roshiago	ロシア語	Russian
Supeingo	スペイン語	Spanish
mō ichido	もう一度	once again, one more time
sukoshi	少し	a little
yukkuri	ゆっくり	slowly
wakaru / wakarimasu	分かる/分かります	understand

Culture and vocabulary notes

The suffix **-go** means "language." The verb **wakaru / wakarimasu** in Sentence Pattern 32 means "understand," "grasp," or "get." What is understood is indicated by the particle **ga**.

Grammar

Sentence Pattern 32	
NOUN + **ga / wakarimasu ka?** NOUN + が分かりますか？	Do you understand + NOUN?

Examples

Nihongo ga wakarimasu ka? 日本語が分かりますか？	Do you understand Japanese?

Eigo ga wakarimasu ka?   Do you understand English?
英語が分かりますか？

Furansugo ga wakarimasu ka?   Do you understand French?
フランス語が分かりますか？

Recall and compare:

Tanaka-san wa tenisu ga jōzu desu.   Miss Tanaka is good at tennis.
田中さんはテニスが上手です。

Sumisu-san wa Nihongo ga wakarimasu.   Mr. Smith understands Japanese.
スミスさんは日本語が
　分かります。

Sumisu-san wa Nihongo o hanashimasu.   Mr. Smith speaks Japanese.
スミスさんは日本語を話します。

Practice

Practice the saying the following short dialogues aloud.

Nihongo o hanashimasu ka?   Do you speak Japanese?
日本語を話しますか？

Sukoshi hanashimasu.   I speak very little.
すこし話します。

Yukkuri hanashite kudasai.   Please speak slowly.
ゆっくり話してください。

Furansugo ga wakarimasu ka?   Do you understand French?
フランス語が分かりますか？

Iie, wakarimasen.   No, I don't.
いいえ、分かりますせん。

Nihongo o hanashite kudasai.   Please speak Japanese.
日本語を話してください。

Wakarimashita ka?   Did you understand?
分かりましたか？

Iie, wakarimasen deshita.   No, I didn't.
いいえ、分かりますせんでした。

Mō ichido itte kudasai.   Please say it once again.
もう一度言ってください。

Seeking Advice

In this lesson you will learn how to ask where to find a certain type of place, such as a restaurant that serves tasty food.

Vocabulary

benri (na)	便利な	convenient
dokoka	どこか	somewhere
oshieru / oshiemasu	教える/教えます	to teach, inform, tell
tokoro	所	place, spot

Culture and vocabulary notes

Dokoka is a rather flexible word. Note and try out the various translations in the practice section below. **Oshiete kudasai** is a polite way of asking someone for information. It can also mean, "please teach me," as in **Nihongo o oshiete kudasai**, "Please teach me Japanese."

Grammar

Sentence Pattern 30C	
Dokoka / + KIND OF PLACE + o / oshiete kudasai. どこか + KIND OF PLACE + を教えてください。	Please tell me of a + KIND OF PLACE + somewhere.
Dokoka benri na kissaten o oshiete kudasai. どこか便利な喫茶店を教えて ください。	Please tell me of a convenient coffee shop somewhere.

Practice

1. Practice repeating the following sentences aloud and then try making some others of your own.

Dokoka yasui resutoran o oshiete kudasai.
どこか安いレストランを教え
てください。

Please tell me where an inexpensive restaurant is.

Dokoka ii depāto o oshiete kudasai.
どこかいいデパートを教えて
ください。

Please tell me where a good department store might be.

Dokoka chikai kissaten o oshiete kudasai.
どこか近い喫茶店を教えて
ください。

Please tell me (where I can find) a coffee shop nearby.

Dokoka oishii resutoran o oshiete kudasai.
どこかおいしいレストランを
教えてください。

Please tell me where a restaurant with good food is.

Dokoka benri na eki o oshiete kudasai.
どこか便利な駅を教えて
ください。

Please tell me where a convenient train station is.

Dokoka shizuka na resutoran o oshiete kudasai.
どこか静かなレストランを
教えてください。

Please tell me of a quiet restaurant somewhere.

Doing What the Teacher Tells You

In this lesson, you will learn some requests, such as those you might hear in a Japanese classroom.

Vocabulary

doa	ドア	door
hon	本	book
mado	窓	window
namae	名前	name
akeru / akemasu	開ける/開けます。	open
shimeru / shimemasu	閉める/閉めます	close

Grammar

If you are in a classroom situation, you might be called upon by the teacher to do some of the following.

Hon o yonde kudasai.
本を読んでください。
Please read the book.

Kore o shite kudasai.
これをしてください。
Please do this (problem).

Mado o shimete kudasai.
窓を閉めてください。
Please close the window.

Doa o shimete kudasai.
ドアを閉めてください。
Please close the door.

Mado o akete kudasai.
窓を開けてください。
Please open the window.

Doa o akete kudasai.
ドアを開けてください。
Please open the door.

Nihongo o hanashite kudasai.
日本語を話してください。
Please speak Japanese.

Nihongo o kaite kudasai.
日本語を書いてください。
Please write in Japanese.

Namae o kaite kudasai.
名前を書いてください。
Please write your name.

Being Very Polite

In this lesson you will learn the very polite forms of some common verbs.

Vocabulary

goran ni naru	御覧になる	to look (very polite)
gozonji	ご存じ	to know (very polite)
irassharu	いらっしゃる	to go; to come (very polite)
meshiagaru	召し上がる	to eat; to drink (very polite)
mesu / o-meshi ni naru	召す/お召しになる	to wear (very polite)
nasaru	なさる	to do (very polite)
ossharu	おっしゃる	to say (very polite)

Culture and vocabulary notes

Some Japanese words and constructions are inherently polite. The extremely polite forms of verbs that you will learn here (also called honorific verbs) do not differ in meaning from the polite forms that you have already learned. But they do differ in the degree of politeness that both speaker and listener attach to them. Since their proper use requires some feeling for Japanese social situations, concentrate here on understanding rather than learning to speak these forms. As a guest in Japan you will likely hear them often.

Grammar

Compare the following normal-polite and extremely polite expressions.

Extremely Polite	Polite	
Dōzo meshiagatte kudasai. どうぞ召し上がって ください。	**Dōzo tabete kudasai.** どうぞ食べて ください。	Please eat (or drink).
	Dōzo nonde kudasai. どうぞ飲んで ください。	

Dōzo goran kudasai.
どうぞ御覧ください。

Dōzo mite kudasai.
どうぞ見てくださ
い。

Please look.

Dōzo irasshatte kudasai.
どうぞいらっしゃって
ください。

Dōzo itte kudasai.
どうぞ行って
ください。

Please go (or come).

Dōzo kite kudasai.
どうぞ来て
ください。

Dōzo nasatte kudasai.
どうぞなさって
ください。

Dōzo shite kudasai.
どうぞして
ください。

Please do (it).

Dōzo o-agari kudasai.
どうぞお上がり
ください。

Dōzo agatte kudasai.
どうぞ上がって
ください。

Please come up.

Dōzo o-hairi kudasai.
どうぞお入り
ください。

Dōzo haitte kudasai.
どうぞ入って
ください。

Please come in.

Dōzo o-machi kudasai.
どうぞお待ち
ください。

Dōzo matte kudasai.
どうぞ待って
ください。

Please wait.

Dōzo o-meshi kudasai.
どうぞお召し
ください。

Dōzo kite kudasai.
どうぞ着て
ください。

Please wear (it).

Dōzo osshatte kudasai.
どうぞおっしゃって
ください。

Dōzo itte kudasai.
どうぞ言って
ください。

Please say (it).

Going to the Beauty Parlor or the Barber

In this lesson you will learn vocabulary and expressions that are often used in beauty parlors or barber shops.

Vocabulary

Barber- and Beauty Parlor-Related Expressions

heyādai	ヘヤーダイ	hairdye
higesori	髭剃り	shave
kariageru / kariagemasu	刈り上げる/刈り上げます	to clip the hair
katto	カット	haircut
kōrudo pāma	コールドパーマ	cold wave
manikyua	マニキュア	manicure
mijikaku	短く	short
rezā katto	レザーカット	razor cut
shanpū	シャンプー	shampoo
suku / sukimasu	すく/すきます	to thin the hair
suso	すそ	(trim) the ends
sutairu	スタイル	style, hairstyle

Other Vocabulary

chōdo	ちょうど	exactly
dake	だけ	only
Donna?	どんな	What kind of?
o-azukari shimasu	お預かりします	to keep; take care of
ōbā	オーバー	overcoat
o-tsuri	おつり	change (money)
sebiro	背広	man's jacket
shōshō	少々	a little; a bit
uwagi	上着	jacket

Useful Expressions

(Kōto o) o-azukari shimasu. （コートを）お預かりします。	Let me take (your coat).
O-machidōsama deshita. お街度様でした。	Thank you for waiting.
Shōshō o-machi kudasai. 少々お待ちください。	Kindly wait a short while.

Culture and vocabulary notes

A beauty parlor in Japanese is called **biyōin**. Barber shops are known by various names: **rihatsuten, tokoya, sanpatsuya,** and **bābā-shoppu. Bābā-shoppu** is most often used in Western-style hotels. Barbers can be called **riyōshi, rihatsushi,** or **tokoya. Riyōshi** is the word most commonly used nowadays.

The word **mijikaku** is an adverb that tells how you want your hair to be cut or clipped. It is formed from the adjective **mijikai** (learned in Chapter 5) by removing the final -i and adding -ku to the adjective stem. The addition of **arimasen** to this adverb form will produce the polite present-negative adjective form.

Grammar

The following shows what might happen when you enter a barber shop or a beauty parlor. The barber or beautician will speak to you very politely (as will all people who wait on you in Japan). Learn some of the polite phrases here for recognition and practice some of the requests using words in the above vocabulary list.

Barber (or Beautician):

Irasshaimase. いらっしゃいませ！	Welcome!

When the chairs are occupied:

Shōshō o-machi kudasai. 少々お待ちください。	Kindly wait a short while.

When it is not crowded:

Kochira e dōzo. こちらへどうぞ。	This way, please.

If you are wearing a coat or jacket, the barber will often offer to take it and hang it up.

Kōto o o-azukari shimasu.   Let me take your coat.
コートをお預かりします。

Then:

Donna sutairu ni shimashō ka?   What style would you like?
どんなスタイルにしましょうか？

Practice some answers to this question, as follows:

Shanpū to setto o shite kudasai.   Please give me a shampoo.
シャンプーとセットをしてください。

Katto o shite kudasai.   Please give me a haircut.
カットをしてください。

Rezā-katto o shite kudasai.   Please give me a razor cut.
レザーカットをしてください。

Mijikaku katto o shite kudasai.   Please cut it short.
短くカットをしてください。

Mijikaku kariagete kudasai.   Please clip it short.
短く刈り上げてください。

Suso dake o-negai shimasu.   Just a trim, please.
すそだけお願いします。

Suite kudasai.   Please thin it out.
すいてください。

Kōrudo pāma o o-negai shimasu.   Please give me a cold wave.
コールドパーマをお願いします。

Heyādai o o-negai shimasu.   Please dye my hair.
ヘヤーダイをお願いします。

When s/he is done, the barber or hair stylist will probably say something like:

Hai, o-machidōsama deshita.   Thank you for sitting
はい、お待ち堂様でした。   (waiting) patiently.

Nisen-gohyaku-en itadakimasu.   That will be ¥2,500.
2,500円いただきます。

If you give him or her the exact amount he will say:

Chōdo o-azukari shimasu.　　　　That's the correct amount.
ちょうどお預かりします。

If you give him or her a ¥10,000 bill:

Ichiman-en o-azukari shimasu.　　That's ¥10,000.
10,000円お預かりします。

Nana-sen-go-hyaku-en no o-tsuri desu.　Here's your change, ¥7,500.
7,500円のおつりです。

And always, before you leave, he and the other employees will give you a hearty thank-you.

Arigatō gozaimashita!　　　　Thank you!
ありがとうございました！

THE VERB -TE FORM

In Chapter 7 you learned how to build the -**masu** form from the dictionary form of the verb. Here you will learn how to make the -**te** form. Together, these two sections will provide you with a valuable reference should you wish to expand your usage and vocabulary while in Japan. After some use and practice, these verb forms should come quite naturally to you.

Recall that there are three types of verbs in Japanese:
1. The vowel verbs, ending in **e** or **i** + **ru**
2. The consonant verbs, ending in -**ku**, -**gu**, -**bu**, -**mu** -**nu**; a vowel + **ru**; a vowel +**u**; -**su**; -**tsu**
3. The irregular verbs, **suru** and **kuru**

1. The Vowel Verb

For the -**te** form of a vowel verb, change the final **ru** into **te** as shown in the following examples:

-eru	taberu	tabete		-iru	miru	mite

2. The Consonant Verb

For the -**te** form of a consanant verb, change the final:

-tsu	→	-tte	matsu	→	matte
vowel + ru	→	-tte	kaeru	→	kaette
vowel + u	→	vowel + -tte	kau	→	katte
-su	→	-shite	hanasu	→	hanashi
-ku*	→	-ite	kaku	→	kaite
-gu	→	-ide	isogu	→	isoide
-bu	→	-nde	yobu	→	yonde
-mu	→	-nde	nomu	→	nonde
-nu	→	-nde	shinu	→	shinde

* iku, "go," is irregular: **itte**.

3. The Irregular Verb

Memorize the -**te** forms of **suru** and **kuru**, shown below.

suru	shite		kuru	kite

Chapter 10
(Lessons 43 – 46)

POLITE SITUATIONS COVERED IN CHAPTER 10

Lesson 43: Greeting your Friends
1. Meeting Someone for the First Time
2. Introducing Two People to Each Other

Lesson 44: Greeting your Friends (continued)
1. Greetings on the Street
2. Visiting a Friend at Home
3. Meeting Someone on the Street
4. Greeting the Teacher
5. In the Living Room at the Tanaka's

Lesson 45: Rising to the Occasion
1. Requesting Something of Your Assistant
2. Keeping a Friend Waiting
3. Receiving a Gift
4. On the Telephone
5. Thanking Your Friend for Helping You the Day Before

Lesson 46: Eating at Someone Else's Home
1. Being Served Tea
2. Mrs. Tanaka Brings Tea and Cake
3. At the Dinner Table

This chapter presents many of the polite words and phrases that the Japanese use when greeting others, when saying thank-you, when apologizing, and when being a guest or a host. Some of these are formula phrases said only at certain times; others can be used in almost any situation.

Brief dialogues follow the vocabulary lists to give you some idea as to when and how these phrases are used, but the best practice situations are on the streets of any Japanese city or town. The expressions you learn here will do wonders for improving your stay in Japan, and you are encouraged to use them often.

DIALOGUE
道で歩いています：
中村：山下さん、お久しぶりですね。
山下：やあ、暫くでしたね.。中村さんはお元気ですか？
中村：おかげさまで。山下さんは？
山下：私も元気です。中村さん、こちらは上田さんです。
　　　上田さん、こちらは中村さんです。
上田：初めまして、どうぞよろしく。
中村：どうぞよろしく。上田さんは学生ですか？
上田：いいえ、会社員です。私の名刺をどうぞ。
中村：ああ、トヨタに勤めていますね。私の名刺をどうぞ。
上田：ああ、英語の先生ですね。私の英語はぜんぜんだめ
　　　です。
山下：えっと、上田さんと私はこれから飲みますが、一緒
　　　に行きませんか？
中村：いいですね。一緒に行きましょう。
上田：ビールを飲みながら英語を教えてください！
山下：でも今は勉強を忘れて、楽しみましょう。
上田：そうですね。楽しみましょう！あそこに行きましょう。

居酒屋で：
ホステス　　：いらしゃいまっせ！少々（を）待ちください。
　　　　　　　こちらへ来てください。
ウエイトレス：何にしましょうか？

山下　　　：ビールを三杯ください。
ウエイトレス：はい、かしこまりました。
山下　　　：今日は上田さんのお誕生日ですから、
　　　　　　乾杯しましょう。
中村　　　：ああそうですか？おめでとうございます！
上田　　　：ありがとうございます。では乾杯！

Walking down the street:

Nakamura:	Yamashita-san, o-hisashiburi desu ne.	Mr. Yamashita, it's been a long time since I saw you last.
Yamashita:	Yā, shibaraku deshita ne. Nakamura-san wa o-genki desu ka?	Hi! It has been a long while, hasn't it? How are you feeling, Mr. Nakamura?
Nakamura:	Okagesama de. Yamashita-san wa?	I'm fine, thanks. How about you, Mr. Yamashita?
Yamashita:	Watashi mo genki desu. Nakamura-san, kochira wa Ueda-san desu. Ueda-san, kochira wa Nakamura-san desu.	I'm fine too. Mr. Nakamura, this is Miss Ueda. Miss Ueda, this is Mr. Nakamura.
Ueda :	Hajimemashite. Dōzo yoroshiku.	How do you do? I'm happy to meet you.
Nakamura:	Dōzo yoroshiku. Ueda-san wa gakusei desu ka?	I'm pleased to meet you. Are you a student, Miss Ueda?
Ueda :	Iie, kaisha-in desu. Watashi no meishi o dōzo.	No, I'm a company employee. Here's my name card.
Nakamura:	Ā, Toyota de tsutomete imasu ne. Watashi no meishi o dōzo.	Oh, I see you work for Toyota. Here's my name card.
Ueda :	Ā, eigo no sensei desu ne. Watashi no eigo wa zenzen dame desu.	Oh, I see you are an English teacher. My English is terrible.
Yamashita:	Etto, Ueda-san to watashi wa kore kara nomimasu ga, issho ni ikimasen ka?	Say, Miss Ueda and I were just going out for a drink. Won't you come along with us?
Nakamura:	Ii desu ne. Issho ni ikimashō.	That sounds good. Sure, let's go.
Ueda :	Biiru o nominagara, eigo o oshiete kudasai!	While we drink some beer, please teach us some English!

| Yamashita: | Demo ima wa benkyō o wasurete, tanoshimimashō. | Oh, let's forget about studying now and have some fun! |
| Ueda : | Sō desu ne. Tanoshimimashō! Asoko ni ikimashō. | Okay. Let's have fun! Let's go to that place (over there). |

At a pub:

Hostess :	Irashimasse! Shōshō (o) machi kudasai.	Welcome! Please wait a moment. (A few minutes later)
	Kochira e kite kudasai.	Please come this way.
Waitress :	Nani ni shimashō ka?	What would you like?
Yamashita :	Biiru o san-bai kudasai.	Three glasses of beer please.
Waitress :	Hai, kashikomarimashita.	Okay, just as you've ordered it, sir.
Yamashita :	Kyō wa Ueda-san no o-tanjōbi desu kara, kanpai shimashō!	Today is Miss Ueda's birthday, so let's make a toast!
Nakamura :	Ā sō desu ka? Omedetō gozaimasu!	Oh, really? Congratulations!
Ueda :	Arigatō gozaimasu. Dewa kanpai!	Thank you. Well then, cheers!

Dialogue vocabulary

dame	だめ	bad; wrong
dōzo yoroshiku.	どうぞよろしく	I'm happy to meet you.
hajimemashite	初めまして	How do you do?
kaisha-in	会社員	company employee
Kanpai!	乾杯！	Cheers! Bottoms up!
kanpai suru	乾杯する	to make a toast
kashikomarimashita	かしこまりました	as you request, sir (ma'am)
meishi	名刺	business card
o-hisashiburi	お久しぶり	a long time
okagesama de	おかげさまで	I'm fine, thanks.
shibaraku	暫く	a long time
Tanoshimimashō!	楽しみましょう	Let's have fun!
zenzen	ぜんぜん	completely

Culture and vocabulary notes

Both **o-hisashiburi** and **shibaraku** are common greetings between friends or acquaintances who haven't met for some time. **Meishi**, or business cards, are commonly exchanged between business people at the time they first meet. Such a card typically includes the person's name, company, and position among other information. This helps to establish the relative status of the people exchanging the cards and thus the degree of politeness that each should use in their conversations with one another.

Hajimemashite, meaning *I am meeting you for the first time,* is a very common greeting upon first meeting someone. **Dōzo yoroshiku**, which literally means *Please be good to me,* is often translated as *Nice to meet you.* It is somewhat less formal than **hajimemashite**. The two expressions are often combined during introductions as **Hajimemashite, dōzo yoroshiku**.

Hai (bai, pai) is the counter for containers, such as cups, bowls, or glasses. **Kashikomarimashita** is an extremely polite expression sometimes used by service people to indicate that they will do their best to carry out the request or instructions that they have just received.

The use of a verb stem plus the suffix **nagara** means *while ~ing.* Thus, **shinagara** means *while doing.* It is used to show that two actions take place at the same time.

Greeting Your Friends

In this lesson you will learn how to greet someone that you just met and how to introduce two people to one another. You will also learn some common greetings among friends.

Vocabulary

Kochira wa
こちら
This (person here)

Achira wa
あちら
That (person over there)

Hajimemashite.
初めまして。
How do you do?

(Watakushi wa) Ikeda desu.
(私は) 池田です。
I am Mr. (Mrs., Miss, or Ms.) Ikeda. (very polite)

(Watashi wa) Ikeda desu.
(私は) 池田です。
I am Mr. Ikeda. (polite)

(Watashi) Ikeda desu.
(私) 池田です。
I am Mr. Ikeda. (informal)

Dōzo yoroshiku.
どうぞよろしく。
I am happy to meet you.

O-genki desu ka?
お元気ですか？
How are you?

Ikaga desu ka?
いかがですか？
How are you?

Genki desu.
元気です。
I'm fine.

Okagesama de.
おかげさまで。
I'm fine, thanks.

Aikawarazu.
相変わらず。
As usual. Same as always.

Anata wa?
あなたは？
And you?

Tanaka-san wa? 田中さんは？	And you, Mr Tanaka?
Ohayō gozaimasu. おはようございます。	Good morning. (polite)
Ohayō. おはよう。	Good morning. (informal)
Konnichi wa. こんにちは。	Good afternoon. Hi!
Konban wa. こんばんは。	Good evening.
O-genki de. お元気で。	Take care.
O-yasumi nasai. お休みなさい。	Good night. (polite)
O-yasumi. お休み。	Good night. (informal)
Sayōnara. さようなら。	Good-bye.
meishi 名刺	business card

Culture and vocabulary notes

It is polite and quite common to use directional words such as **kochira** and **achira** when introducing people, as in **Kochira wa Tanaka-san desu**.

The sentence **Watashi Ikeda desu** shows that in colloquial speech the particle **wa** can be omitted.

The polite prefix **o-** in **o-genki** must be used when asking about another's health. But it should be omitted when you are speaking of your own condition, as in **Genki desu**.

Practice

Read over the following short dialogues and then practice saying them aloud. You will have many chances to hear and repeat these phrases in Japan.

1. Meeting Someone for the First Time

Ms. Tanaka:

Hajimemashite. Watakushi wa Tanaka desu.　How do you do?
初めまして。私は田中です。　　　　　　　I am Ms. Tanaka.
Dōzo yoroshiku.　　　　　　　　　　　　　I am happy to meet you.
どうぞよろしく。

Mr. Yamada:

Hajimemashite. Watakushi wa Yamada desu.　How do you do?
初めまして。私は山田です。　　　　　　　I am Mr. Yamada.
Dōzo yoroshiku.　　　　　　　　　　　　　I am happy to meet you.
どうぞよろしく。

2. Introducing Two People to Each Other

When being introduced to someone, Japanese people like to learn not only the person's name but also his title and professional affiliation. Providing this information is the major function of the name card (**meishi**) that you will often be given in Japan. It would be helpful for you to have some name cards of your own, with one side in Japanese and the other in English, giving your professional title, if any, your organization, and your position within it.

Mr. Kobayashi:

Tanaka-san, kochira wa Yamada-san desu.　Ms. Tanaka, this is Mr Ya-
田中さん、こちらは山田さんです。　　　　mada.
Yamada-san, kochira wa Tanaka-san desu.　Mr. Yamada, this is Ms.
山田さん、こちらは田中さんです。　　　　Tanaka.

Mr. Yamada:

Hajimemashite. Dōzo yoroshiku.　　　　　How do you do? I am happy
初めまして。どうぞよろしく。　　　　　　to meet you.

Ms. Tanaka:

Hajimemashite. Dōzo yoroshiku.　　　　　How do you do? I am happy
初めまして。どうぞよろしく。　　　　　　to meet you.

Greeting Your Friends *(continued)*

In this lesson you will learn some additional greetings and some expressions to use when departing. Most of these expressions are very common and you will hear them frequently.

Vocabulary

Greetings

Irasshaimase! いらっしゃいませ！	Welcome! Hello! (very polite)
Irasshai! いらっしゃい！	Welcome! Hello!
Yoku irasshaimashita. よくいらっしゃいました。	Hello! I'm glad you could come.
Gomen kudasai. ごめんください。	Excuse me. (used by a visitor to attract attention)
O-jama shimasu. お邪魔します。	I'm here. (Literally, I'm going to disturb you.)
O-jama shimashita. お邪魔しました。	Excuse me for having disturbed you.
O-jama de itashimasu . . . お邪魔でいたします。	Excuse me, but. . . (very polite; often used by service people)
Shibaraku deshita. 暫くでした。	It's been a long time since I saw you last. (polite)
Shibaraku. 暫く。	It's been a long time since I saw you last. (informal)
Itte mairimasu. 行って参ります。	I'm going now (but will return). (formal)
Itte kimasu. 行って来ます。	I'm going now (but will return). (informal)
Itterasshai. (Itte irasshai.) いってらっしゃい。 （行っていらっしゃい。）	Have a good time. Hurry back.

Mata irasshai. またいらっしゃい。	Please come again.
Mata dōzo. またどうぞ。	Please come again.
Tadaima. ただいま。	I'm home! I've returned.
O-kaeri nasai. お帰りなさい。	Welcome back. (formal)
O-kaeri. お帰り。	Welcome back. (informal)
Yā! やあ！	Hi! (informal)

Other Vocabulary

Māmā desu. まあまあです。	I'm so-so.
mina-san 皆さん	everyone
sensei 先生	teacher

Culture and vocabulary notes

O-jama shimasu literally means "I'm going to disturb you," and it is often used when entering someone else's home or a room in which others are present. **O-jama shimashita** is often used when departing from someone's home or a room in which people are present.

Almost everyone in Japan who leaves his or her home to go to school, to work, to the store, and so on, says **Itte kimasu**, "I'm going now (but will return)," when s/he leaves. Anyone who sees him/her off invariably says **Itte-rasshai**, "Have a good time, hurry back" (literally, "Go and please come back"). When the person who has been away returns, s/he says **Tadaima**, "I'm back." Those who greet him/her upon his/her return say **O-kaeri nasai**, "Welcome home." You will find that you often hear these four expressions.

Japanese people generally prefer to call a person with whom they are speaking by his or her last name instead of using **anata**, "you."

Practice

Read over the following short dialogues and then practice saying them aloud.
You will hear and repeat these phrases often in Japan.

1. Greetings on the Street

Mr. Takahashi:
Yā, shibaraku.　　　　　　　　　Hi! It's been a long time
やあ、暫く。　　　　　　　　　　　since I saw you last.

Mr. Koyama:
Shibaraku deshita ne.　　　　　　Yes, it's been a long time
暫くでしたね。　　　　　　　　　since I saw you last.
O-genki desu ka?　　　　　　　　How are you?
お元気ですか？

Mr. Takahashi:
Okagesama de.　　　　　　　　　I'm fine, thanks.
おかげさまで。
Koyama-san wa?　　　　　　　　How about you?
小山さんは？

Mr. Koyama:
Ē, okagesama de.　　　　　　　　Yes, I'm fine, thanks.
ええ、おかげさまで。

2. Visiting a Friend at Home

Ms. Yamada:
Gomen kudasai.　　　　　　　　Excuse me.
ごめんください。

Ms. Tanaka:
Hai, donata desu ka?　　　　　　Yes, who is it?
はい、どなたですか？

Ms. Yamada:

Yamada desu.　　　　　　　　　　　　　　It's Yamada.
山田です。

Ms. Tanaka:

Ā, chotto matte kudasai. [or]　　　　　　Yes, just a moment, please.
ああ、ちょっと待ってください。　　　　　(Opening the door)
Ā, chotto o-machi kudasai.
ああ、ちょっとお待ちください。
Irasshaimase. Dōzo, dōzo.　　　　　　　Welcome! Please come in.
いらっしゃいませ。どうぞ。どうぞ。

Ms. Yamada:

Konban wa.　　　　　　　　　　　　　　Good evening.
こんばんは。

Ms. Tanaka:

Konban wa. Sā, kochira e.　　　　　　　Good evening. Well, please
こんばんは。さあ、こちらへ。　　　　　　come this way.

3. Meeting Someone on the Street

Mr. Tanaka:

Konnichi wa.　　　　　　　　　　　　　Good afternoon.
こんにちは。

Mr. Yamada:

Ā, konnichi wa. O-genki desu ka?　　　Oh, good afternoon.
ああ、こんにちは。お元気ですか？　　　How are you?

Mr. Tanaka:

Okagesama de. Yamada-san wa?　　　　I'm fine thanks.
おかげさまで。山田さんは？　　　　　　How about you?

Mr. Yamada:

Hai, okagesama de.　　　　　　　　　　Yes, I'm fine thanks.
はい、おかげさまで。

4. Greeting the Teacher

Since the relationship between a teacher and his students is considered a formal one, polite forms of greeting (For example, **ohayō gozaimasu** rather than **ohayō**) are used.

Teacher:

Minasan, ohayō gozaimasu.　　　　　Good morning, everyone.
皆さん、おはようございます。

Students:

Yamada Sensei, ohayō gozaimasu.　　Good morning, Mr. Yamada.
山田先生、おはようございます。

5. In the Living Room at the Tanaka's

Mr. Tanaka:

Yā, irasshai!　　　　　　　　　　Oh, welcome!
やあ、いらっしゃい！

Mr. Yamada:

Ojama shimasu.　　　　　　　　　Excuse me (for disturbing you).
お邪魔します。

Mr. Tanaka:

O-genki desu ka?　　　　　　　　How are you?
お元気ですか？

Mr. Yamada:

Okagesama de.　　　　　　　　　I'm fine, thanks.
おかげさまで。

Tanaka-san wa?　　　　　　　　　How about you?
田中さんは？

Mr. Tanaka:

Māmā desu.　　　　　　　　　　I'm fine (so-so).
まあまあです。

Rising to the Occasion

In this lesson you will learn a variety of expressions for saying *Thank you, Please, I'm sorry,* and *Congratulations.* In addition, you will learn several other common polite expressions.

Vocabulary

Sumimasen. すみません。	I'm sorry. Thank you for your trouble.
Chotto sumimasen ga . . . ちょっとすみませんが。。。	Excuse me, but. . .
Gomen nasai. ごめんなさい。	Excuse me. Pardon me.
Shitsurei shimasu. 失礼します。	Excuse me. (polite); I must be going.
Shitsurei shimashita. 失礼しました。	Excuse me (for being rude). (referring to a past event)
Shitsurei. 失礼。	Excuse me. (informal); rudeness
Dōzo. どうぞ。	Please. (offering something)
O-negai shimasu. お願いします。	Please. (requesting something)
Dōmo arigatō gozaimasu. どうもありがとうございます。	Thank you very much.
Arigatō gozaimasu. ありがとうございます。	Thank you.
Arigatō gozaimashita. ありがとうございました。	Thank you. (referring to a past event)
Arigatō. ありがとう。	Thank you. (informal)
Dōmo. どうも。	Thanks. (informal)

Dō itashimashite.
どういたしまして。

Don't mention it.

Iie, dō itashimashite.
いいえ、どういたしまして。

No, not at all. That's all right.

Moshi-moshi.
もしもし。

Hello. (telephone only)

Dōmo. O-matase itashimashita.
どうも。お待たせいたしました。

I am sorry to have kept you waiting. (very polite)

O-machidōsama deshita.
お待ち堂様でした。

I am sorry to have kept you waiting. (polite)

O-machidōsama.
お待ち堂様。

Thank you for waiting. I'm sorry to have kept you waiting. (informal)

Shōshō, o-machi kudasai.
少々お待ちください。

Just a moment, please. (polite)

Chotto matte kudasai.
ちょっと待ってください。

Just a moment. (informal)

O-saki ni.
お先に。

Excuse me for going first.

Dōzo, o-saki ni.
どうぞ、お先に。

Please go ahead. After you.

Hai, kashikomarimashita.
はい、かしこまりました。

As you request, sir (ma'am).

Omedetō gozaimasu.
おめでとうございます。

Congratulations! (polite)

Omedetō.
おめでとう。

Congratulations! (informal)

Go-kekkon omedetō gozaimasu.
ご結婚おめでとうございます。

Congratulations on your marriage!

Go-kon'yaku omedetō gozaimasu.
ご婚約おめでとうございます。

Congratulations on your engagement!

Go-shūshoku omedetō gozaimasu.
ご就職おめでとうございます。

Congratulations on your new job!

Go-sotsugyō omedetō gozaimasu.
ご卒業おめでとうございます。

Congratulations on your graduation!

Culture and vocabulary notes

Sumimasen can be used as an apology. It can also be used to express thanks to someone who has done something on your behalf.

Shitsurei shimasu is used when excusing yourself from a room. **Shitsurei shimashita** (literally, "I committed a rudeness") is used as an apology for something you've done.

Practice

Read over the following short dialogues covering various situations and then practice saying them aloud.

1. Requesting Something of Your Assistant

You:

Kore o onegai shimasu.   I'd like you to do this.
これをお願いします。

Assistant:

Hai. (Kashikomarimashita.)   Yes, sir (ma'am, etc.).
はい。（かしこまりました。）

2. Keeping a Friend Waiting

You:

O-machidōsama deshita.   I'm sorry to have kept you waiting.
お待ち堂様でした。

Friend:

(Iie,) dō itashimashite.   No, not at all.
（いいえ、）どういたしまして。

3. Receiving a Gift

You:

Dōmo arigatō gozaimasu.   Thank you very much.
どうもありがとうございます。

Friend:
Dō itashimashite. You're welcome.
どういたしまして。

4. On the Telephone

You (picking up the telephone):
Moshi-moshi. Hello?
もしもし。

Person calling:
Yamada-san wa irasshaimasu ka? Is Mrs. Yamada there?
(**Irasshaimasu** is a polite form of **imasu**.)
山田さんはいらっしゃいますか？

You:
Shōshō, o-machi kudasai. Just a moment, please.
少々お待ちください。

5. Thanking Your Friend for Helping You the Day Before

You:
Kinō wa dōmo arigatō gozaimashita. Thank you very much for
昨日はどうもありがとうございま (what you did) yesterday.
した。

Friend:
Dō itashimashite. You're welcome.
どういたしまして。

Eating at Someone Else's Home

In this final lesson, you will learn several expressions related to serving and accepting food and drinks.

Vocabulary

Ikaga? いかが	How about?
ippai 一杯	one cup; one glass
kekkō 結構	plenty, sufficient
mō もう	more; another
somatsu 祖末	cheap; shabby
totemo とても	very
Kōhii wa ikaga desu ka? コーヒーはいかがですか？	How about some coffee?
O-cha wa ikaga? お茶はいかが？	How about tea?
O-cha o mō ippai ikaga? お茶をもう一杯いかが？	How about another cup of tea?
O-cha o mō ippai dōzo. お茶をもう一杯どうぞ。	Please have another cup of tea.
Hai, itadakimasu. はい、いただきます。	Yes, thank you. (I'll have some.)
Iie, kekkō desu. いいえ、結構です。	No, thank you. (I've had plenty.)
Totemo oishikatta desu. とてもおいしかったです。	It was very delicious.
Gochisōsama deshita. 御馳走さまでした。	Thank you for the food (meal).

Gochisōsama. 御馳走さま。	Thank you for the food. (informal)
O-somatsusama deshita. お粗末様でした。	It was nothing.

Culture and vocabulary notes

In **O-cha o mō ippai ikaga?** the word **mō** means "another," and **ikaga** is a polite word for "how" or "how about." **Ippai**, "a cup," is a combination of **ichi**, "one," and **-hai**, the counter for cups or glasses (**ippai**, **nihai**, **sanbai**, etc.).

When you are a guest in Japan, you should always say **Itadakimasu** before eating the food—be it a meal or snack—that is offered to you. After finishing, you should say **Gochisōsama deshita** to show your appreciation to the host and hostess.

Practice

Read over the following short dialogues concerning various situations related to offering and receiving food and drink. Then practice saying them aloud.

1. Being Served Tea

Hostess:

Dōzo. どうぞ。	Please (have this).

You:

Arigatō gozaimasu. Itadakimasu. ありがとうございます。 　いただきます。	Thank you. I'll have it.

Hostess:

O-cha o mō ippai ikaga? お茶をもう一杯いかが？	How about another cup of tea?

You:

Ē, itadakimasu. ええ、いただきます。	Yes, thank you . . .

Gochisōsama deshita.
  Totemo oishikatta desu.
御馳走さまでした。
  とてもおいしかったです。

Thank you. It was very
  delicious (when finished).

2. Mrs. Tanaka Brings Tea and Cake

Mrs. Tanaka:
O-cha o dōzo.
お茶をどうぞ。

Please have some tea.

You:
Dōmo arigatō gozaimasu.
  Itadakimasu.
どうもありがとうございます。
  いただきます。

Thank you very much.
  I'll have some.

Oishii kēki desu ne.
おいしいケーキですね。

What delicious cake!

Mrs. Tanaka:
O-cha o mō ippai ikaga desu ka?
お茶をもう一杯いかがですか？

How about another cup of tea?

You:
Hā, dōmo.
はあ、どうも。

Oh, thank you.

3. At the Dinner Table

Hostess:
Dōzo takusan meshiagatte kudasai.
どうぞ沢山召し上がって
  ください。

Please eat plenty (very polite).

Guest:
Itadakimasu.
いただきます。

Thank you. I'll have some.

Hostess:

Mō sukoshi ikaga desu ka?
もう少しいかがですか？

How about some more
  (rice, sakē, etc.)?

Guest:

Mō sukoshi itadakimasu. [or]
もう少しいただきます。

Yes, I'll have a little more. [or]

Mō kekkō desu.
もう結構です。

No, thank you. I've had plenty.

Gochisōsama deshita.
  Totemo oishikatta desu.
御馳走さまでした。
  とてもおいしかったです。

Thank you for the meal. It was
  very delicious.

Hostess:

O-somatsusama deshita.
お粗末様でした。

It was nothing, really.

ANSWERS

CHAPTER 1
Page 20
(a) Kōhii o kudasai.
(b) Sandoitchi o kudasai.
(c) Remonēdo o kudasai.
(d) Aisukuriimu sōda o kudasai.
(f) O-cha o kudasai.

Page 22
(a) Biiru o kudasai.
(b) Sukotchi uisukii o mizuwari de kudasai.
(c) Burandē o kudasai.
(d) Sukotchi uisukii o sutorēto de kudasai.

Page 25
(a) Kōhii to kēki o kudasai.
(b) Miruku to hamu sando o kudasai.
(c) Kōhii to sarada o kudasai.
(d) Remonēdo to appuru pai o kudasai.
(e) Jinfuizu to biiru o kudasai.

Page 29
(a) Kono nekutai o kudasai.
(b) Ano sukāfu o kudasai.
(c) Kono fuirumu o kudasai.
(d) Sono kamera o kudasai.
(e) Ano sētā o kudasai.

CHAPTER 2
Page 43
1. Sukiyaki ga tabetai desu ka? Hai (Ē), tabetai desu.
2. Biiru ga nomitai desu ka? Hai (Ē), nomitai desu.
3. Kamera ga kaitai desu ka? Hai (Ē), kaitai desu.
4. Terebi ga mitai desu ka? Hai (Ē), mitai desu.
5. Nihon e ikitai desu ka? Hai (Ē), ikitai desu.

CHAPTER 3
Page 66
(a) Chotto sumimasen ga, eigakan wa dochira desu ka?
(b) Chotto sumimasen ga, kōban wa doko desu ka?
(c) Chotto sumimasen ga, yūbinkyoku wa dochira desu ka?
(d) Chotto sumimasen ga, eki wa doko desu ka?
(e) Chotto sumimasen ga, Tōkyō Eki wa dochira desu ka?
(f) Chotto sumimasen ga, chikatetsu no eki wa dochira desu ka?
(g) Chotto sumimasen ga, takushii noriba wa doko desu ka?
(h) Chotto sumimasen ga, biyōin wa doko desu ka?

Page 74
1. Hai, (kore wa) yūbinkyoku desu. Iie, (kore wa) yūbinkyoku ja arimasen.
2. Hai, (are wa) unagi desu. Iie, (are wa) unagi ja arimasen.
3. Hai, (kore wa) tōfu desu. Iie, (kore wa) tōfu ja arimasen.
4. Hai, (are wa) jinja desu. Iie, (are wa) jinja ja arimasen.
5. Hai, (kore wa) Shinjuku Eki desu. Iie, (kore wa) Shinjuku Eki ja arimasen.
6. Hai, (are wa) Tōdai desu. Iie, (are wa) Tōdai ja arimasen.
7. Hai, (kore wa) basu no noriba desu. Iie, (kore wa) basu no noriba ja arimasen.

CHAPTER 4
Pages 93-94
(a) Boringu o shimashō.
(b) Benkyō o shimashō.
(c) Kyōto e ikimashō.
(d) Sanpo o shimashō.
(e) Tenisu o shimashō.

(f) Gorufu o shimashō.

(g) Renshū o shimashō.

(h) Fuji-san e ikimashō.

(i) Sukiyaki o tabemashō.

(j) Kono kamera o kaimashō.

(k) Ano eiga e ikimashō.

(1) O-sake o nomimashō.

(m) Ano shashin-ya e ikimashō.

(n) Eki e ikimashō.

(o) Kono Kabuki o mimashō.

(p) O-cha o nomimashō.

CHAPTER 5
Page 111

(a) Takai desu ne.

(b) Yasui desu ne.

(c) Ōkii desu ne.

(d) Chiisai desu ne.

(f) Nagai desu ne.

(e) Mijikai desu ne.

Page 133 (1)

(a) Tenpura ga suki desu.

(b) Tanaka-san wa o-sake ga kirai desu.

(c) Haha wa o-ryōri ga jōzu desu.

(d) Chichi wa Eigo ga jōzu desu.

(e) Piano ga heta desu.

Page 133 (2)

(a) Kirei ja arimasen.

(b) Kyōto e ikitaku arimasen.

(c) Omoshiroku arimasen.

(d) Watakushi wa Nihongo ga suki ja arimasen.

(e) Tanoshii eiga ja arimasen deshita.

(f) Satō-san wa genki na hito ja arimasen.

(g) Tōkyō wa shizuka ja arimasen.

(h) Are wa yūbinkyoku ja arimasen.

(1) Sono kamera wa yasuku arimasen deshita.

(j) Yūmei na hito ja arimasen deshita.

Page 134

(a) Unagi teishoku ga tabetai desu.

(b) Tsumetai biiru ga nomitai desu.

(c) Kyōto e ikitai desu.

(d) Haha wa o-ryōri ga jōzu desu.

(e) Piano ga heta desu.

(f) O-sashimi ga kirai desu.

CHAPTER 6
Page 142 (1)

(a) nijū-en

(b) kyūjū-en

(c) hyaku-en

(d) sanbyaku-gojū-en

(e) yonhyaku-yonjū-go-en

(f) roppyaku-nanajū-en

(g) sen-nihyaku-gojū-en

(h) nisen-sanbyaku-rokujū-en

(i) sanzen-gohyaku-en

(j) rokusen-happyaku-kyūjū-en

(k) hassen-roppyaku-nijū-go-en

(l) ichi-man-gohyaku-en

(m) sanman-nanasen-happyaku-kyūjū-kyū-en

(n) roku-man-nisen-sanbyaku-gojū-go-en

Page 142 (2)

(a) Kore wa ikura desu ka?

(b) Ano rajio wa ikura desu ka?

(c) Kono sutereo wa ikura desu ka ?

(d) Teishoku wa ikura desu ka ?

Page 144

1. Otona, ichi-mai.

2. Gakusei, ni-mai.

3. Otona, ni-mai.

4. Kodomo, san-mai; otona, ichi-mai.

5. Otona, ni-mai; gakusei, ichi-mai; kodomo, ni-mai.

6. Gakusei, ichi-mai; kodomo, san-mai.

Page 146

1. Sapporo, gakusei, ichi-mai (kudasai).
2. Nara, ōfuku, ichi-mai (kudasai).
3. Tōkyō, katamichi, ni-mai (kudasai).
4. Kyōto, ōfuku; otona, ichi-mai; gakusei, ni-mai; kodomo, ichi-mai (kudasai).
5. Kamakura, ōfuku, ni-mai (kudasai).

Page 148

(a) Hagaki o go-mai kudasai.
(b) Kōkūshokan o jū-mai kudasai.
(c) Nijū-en kitte o go-mai kudasai.
(d) Hachijū-en kitte o nijū-mai kudasai.
(e) Hyaku-nijū-en kitte o yon-mai kudasai.
(f) Hachijū-en kitte o go-mai to hagaki o jū-mai kudasai.
(g) Nijū-en kitte o nijū-mai to kōkūshokan o go-mai kudasai.

Page 152 (1)

(a) Yo-ji desu.
(b) Shichi-ji desu.
(c) Jūichi-ji-han desu.
(d) Roku-ji-han desu.
(e) Ni-ji-jūgo-fun desu.
(f) San-ji-jūgo-fun desu.
(g) Jūichi-ji desu.
(h) Ku-ji-han desu.
(i) Jū-ji-han desu.
(j) Yo-ji-sanjū-roppun desu.
(k) Go-ji-nijūkyū-fun desu.
(l) Ichi-ji-nana-fun desu.
(m) Roku-ji desu.
(n) Hachi-ji-han desu.
(o) Jūni-ji-sanjūhachi-fun desu.
(p) Roku-ji-yonjūnana-fun desu.
(q) Yo-ji-yonjūgo-fun desu.
(r) Go-ji-sanjūippun desu.
(s) Ichi-ji-han desu.
(t) Shichi-ji-gojuppun desu.
(u) Hachi-ji-gojūgo-fun desu.
(v) Ni-ji-han desu.
(w) San-ji-sanjūyon-pun desu.
(x) Jū-ji-jūsan-pun desu.
(y) Jūichi-ji-sanjūgo-fun desu.

Page 152 (2)

1. Shichi-ji ni ikimashō.
2. Roku-ji-han ni tabemashō.
3. San-ji-han ni ikitai desu.

Page 154 (1)

(a) San nana nana ichi no nana kyū ichi zero
(b) San roku san ichi no ni roku roku ichi
(c) San nana go nana no go yon ichi ichi
(d) San ni roku ichi no zero zero roku ichi
(e) San kyū roku ichi no kyū san yon zero
(f) San hachi zero go no kyū yon nana ichi

Page 154 (2)

(a) Roku roku no san nana hachi yon
(b) Ni san no zero hachi nana ichi
(c) San ni no san roku nana ni
(d) Ni san no yon hachi san hachi

CHAPTER 7
Page 163

(a) Taitei nani o shimasu ka? Tenisu o shimasu.
(b) Ashita nani o shimasu ka?
Kyōto e ikimasu.
(c) Raishū nani o shimasu ka?
Tōkyō e ikimasu.
(d) Rainen nani o shimasu ka?
Itaria e ikimasu.
(e) Kinō nani o shimashita ka?
Terebi o mimashita.
(f) Sengetsu nani o shimashita ka?
Nara e ikimashita.
(g) Kinō nani o kaimashita ka? Sētā o kaimashita.
(h) Kinō doko de sono reinkōto o kaimashita ka? Depāto de kaimashita.
(i) Kinō no yoru nani o mimashita ka?
Nihon no eiga o mimashita.
(j) Kinō doko e ikimashita ka?
Kyōto e ikimashita.
(k) Kesa nani o nomimashita ka?
Kōhii o nomimashita.
(l) Taitei doko de tabemasu ka?
Uchi de tabemasu.

CHAPTER 8
Page 174
(a) Kaki o mittsu kudasai.
(b) Mikan o tō kudasai.
(c) Momo o muttsu kudasai.
(d) Nashi o yottsu kudasai.
(e) Orenji o nanatsu kudasai.
(f) Ringo o yattsu kudasai.
(g) Suika o hanbun kudasai.

Page 178 (1)
(a) Jagaimo o muttsu kudasai.
(b) Kyabetsu o futatsu kudasai.
(c) Nasu o itsutsu kudasai.
(d) Retasu o mittsu kudasai.
(e) Karifurawā o hitotsu kudasai.
(f) Tamanegi o nanatsu kudasai.
(g) Tomato o itsutsu kudasai.

Page 178 (2)
(a) banana hitofusa
(b) ichigo hitohako
(c) tamanegi hitoyama
(d) tomato hitoyama
(e) sakuranbo hitohako
(f) budō futafusa
(g) kaki hitoyama
(h) mikan hitoyama

Page 180
1. Kodomo ga futari imasu.
2. Otona ga san-nin imasu.
3. Gakusei ga go-nin imasu.
4. Sensei ga yo-nin imasu.
5. Amerikajin ga roku-nin imashita.
6. Nihonjin ga hachi-nin imasu ka?

APPENDIX 1

Suplementary vocabulary

Other Useful Borrowed Words

aisu tii	アイスティー	ice tea
būtsu	ブーツ	boots
dōnatsu	ドーナツ	doughnuts
ekonomii kurasu	エコノミークラス	economy class
erebetā	エレベーター	elevator
esukarētā	エスカレーター	escalator
gasorin sutando	ガソリンスタンド	gasoline stand (gas station)
gitā	ギター	guitar
handobaggu	ハンドバッグ	handbag
heā doraiyā	ヘアードライヤー	hairdryer
kasutādo purin	カスタードプリン	custard pudding
kukkii	クッキー	cookies
kurakkā	クラッカー	crackers
mishin	ミシン	sewing machine
ōdoburu	オードブル	appetizer, hors d'oeuvre
orugan	オルガン	organ (musical)
ōtobai	オートバイ	motor bike
pajama	パジャマ	pajamas
ranpu	ランプ	lamp, ramp

rentakā	レンタカー	rent-a-car
sauna	サウナ	sauna bath
shiitsu	シーツ	sheets
taoru	タオル	towel
asuparagasu	アスパラガス	asparagus
burokkori	ブロッコリー	broccoli
guriin piisu	グリーンピース	green peas
kureson	クレソン	watercress
paseri	パセリ	parsley
serori	セロリ	celery

Stores in Japan

bunbōguya	文房具屋	stationery shop
chūka ryōriya	中華料理屋	Chinese restaurant
denkiya	電気屋	electric appliance shop
furuhon-ya	古本屋	second-hand book shop
gofukuya	呉服屋	kimono shop
hanaya	花屋	florist
hon-ya (shoten)	本屋（書店）	book store
kaguya	家具屋	furniture store
kanbutsuya	乾物屋	dry provisions (food) store, grocer
kameraya	カメラ屋	camera shop
kanamonoya	金物屋	hardware store
kudamonoya	果物屋	fruit stand or shop
kusuriya (yakkyoku)	薬屋（薬局）	pharmacy, drugstore
kutsuya	靴屋	shoe store
nikuya	肉屋	meat shop, butcher
o-chaya	お茶屋	tea shop
o-furoya (sentō)	お風呂屋（銭湯）	public bath
o-kashiya	お菓子屋	candy shop
o-mochaya	おもちゃ屋	toy store
o-mochiya	お餅屋	rice-cake store
o-sushiya	お寿司屋	sushi shop
o-tōfu-ya	お豆腐屋	bean-curd shop
pachinkoya	パチンコ屋	pinball parlor
pan-ya	パン屋	bakery
ryokan (yadoya)	旅館（宿屋）	Japanese inn
ryōriya	料理屋	restaurant, eatery
sakanaya	魚屋	fish store
sakaya	酒屋	liquor store, wine seller's
sentakuya (kuriininguya)	洗濯屋（クリーニング屋）	laundry, cleaner
setomonoya	瀬戸物屋	chinaware store
shashin-ya	写真屋	photo studio
shichiya	質屋	pawn shop

shinbun-ya	新聞屋	newspaper stand
sūpāmāketto	スーパーマーケット	supermarket
tabakoya	タバコ屋	cigarette stand
tsukemonoya	漬物屋	pickle shop

Kinship Terms

For You		For Others		Meaning
ani	兄	o-nii-san	お兄さん	older brother
ane	姉	o-nē-san	お姉さん	older sister
otōto	弟	otōto-san	弟さん	younger brother
imōto	妹	imōto-san	妹さん	younger sister
sofu	祖父	o-jii-san	おじいさん	grandfather
sobo	祖母	o-bā-san	おばあさん	grandmother
oji	叔父	oji-san	おじさん	uncle
oba	叔母	oba-san	おばさん	aunt
mago	孫	o-mago-san	お孫さん	grandchild
oi	甥	oigo-san	甥御さん	nephew
mei	姪	meigo-san	姪御さん	niece
itoko	いとこ/従兄弟	o-itoko-san	お従兄弟さん	cousin

Nationalities

Chūgokujin	中国人	Chinese
Doitsujin	ドイツ人	German
Kankokujin	韓国人	Korean
Indojin	インド人	Indian
Roshiajin	ロシア人	Russian

Occupations

bengoshi	弁護士	lawyer
berubōi	ベルボーイ	bell boy
biyōshi	美容師	beautician
daiku	大工	carpenter
gakusha	学者	scholar
geka-i	外科医	surgeon
gishi	技師	engineer
jochū (jochū-san)	女中（女中さん）	maid (in a Japanese inn)
kagakusha	科学者	scientist
kanri-nin	管理人	manager (of an apartment building)
katei kyōshi	家庭教師	private tutor
kenchikuka	建築家	architect
kyōju	教授	professor
o-tetsudai-san	お手伝いさん	housemaid
pōtā (akabō)	ポーター（赤帽）	porter (red cap)
seijika	政治家	politician

sensei	先生	teacher
ikebana no sensei	生け花の先生	flower-arrangement teacher
Nō no sensei	能の先生	Noh theater teacher
o-cha no sensei	お茶の先生	tea-ceremony teacher
odori no sensei	踊りの先生	Japanese-dance teacher
o-koto no sensei	お琴の先生	koto teacher
o-shūji no sensei	お習字の先生	calligraphy teacher
shihai-nin (manējā)	支配人	manager
shikisha	指揮者	conductor (music)
shōbai-nin	商売人	merchant
shōsetsuka	小説家	novelist
sōryo (o-bō-san)	僧侶 (お坊さん)	priest, monk
uētā	ウェイター	waiter
uētoresu	ウェイトレス	waitress

APPENDIX 2

Commonly seen words for recognition

Even if you have not yet studied the Japanese writing system, being able to recognize the following words written in Japanese script and in kanji characters will come in handy, since you will encounter these words frequently.

At a Station

eki	駅	station
iriguchi	入口	entrance
deguchi	出口	exit
kita-guchi	北口	north exit
higashi-guchi	東口	east exit
minami-guchi	南口	south exit
nishi-guchi	西口	west exit
kaisatsu-guchi	改札口	wicket (ticket gate)
midori no madoguchi	みどりの窓口	green ticket window (for reserved seats)
kippu uriba	きっぷ売場	ticket window
kōshū denwa	公衆電話	public telephone
machiai-shitsu	待合室	waiting room
kanko annaijo	観光案内所	tourist information desk
basu annaijo	バス案内所	bus information desk
chikatetsu	地下鉄	subway
takushii	タクシー	taxi
noriba	乗り場	boarding area
akabō	赤帽	red cap

Cities

Tokyo	東京	
Kyoto	京都	
Kamakura	鎌倉	
Nara	奈良	
Osaka	大阪	
Sapporo	札幌	

Facilities

o-tearai, toire	お手洗い、トイレ	toilet
senmenjo	洗面所	washroom
otoko, danshi	男、男子	men
otoko-yu	男湯	men's section of public bath
onna, joshi	女、女子	women
onna-yu	女湯	women's section of public bath

In Town

uketsuke	受付	reception desk
kōban	交番	police substation
byōin	病院	hospital
ginkō	銀行	bank
eigakan	映画館	movie theater
shokudō, resutoran	食堂、レストラン	cafeteria
hoteru	ホテル	hotel
ryokan	旅館	Japanese inn
yūbinkyoku	郵便局	post office
kaisō	回送	in transit (taxi)
kūsha	空車	vacant (taxi)

In a Store

mise	店	shop
esukarētā	エスカレーター	escalator
erebētā	エレベーター	elevator
sēru	セール	sale
tokubai	特売	special offer
osu	押す	push
hiku	引く	pull
en	円	yen (¥)
kinen	禁煙	non-smoking
kitsuen	喫煙	smoking

Numbers

ichi	一	1
ni	二	2
san	三	3
shi	四	4
go	五	5
roku	六	6
nana, shichi	七	7
hachi	八	8
kyū, ku	九	9
jū	十	10
hyaku	百	100
sen	千	1,000
ichiman	万	10,000

APPENDIX 3

False friends

English words whose meanings change after being borrowed into Japanese can give a great deal of trouble unless you are aware of how the meaning has changed. Here is a list of some of these "false friends"—words borrowed from English but having a different meaning in Japanese. English expressions marked with an asterisk are not used in idiomatic English.

Borrowed Word and Meaning in Japanese

Food

			English Word
baikingu	バイキング	all-you-can-eat buffet	Viking
saidā	サイダー	soft drink similar to Seven-Up	cider
sōda	ソーダ	club soda only	soda (of any type)
sunakku	スナック	(1) light meal; (2) small bar or club where drinks and light meals are served	snack

Sports

chansu bōru	チャンスボール	weak return; poor shot	chance ball*
chansu mēkā	チャンスメーカー	heads-up player; player who sparks his team	chance maker*
furu bēsu	フルベース	bases loaded (in baseball)	full base*
ōru sebun	オールセブン	"seven all" (each side has seven points)	all seven*
singuru hitto	シングルヒット	single (in baseball)	single hit*

People

bōi hanto	ボーイハント	"pick up" a boy	boy hunt*
feminisuto	フェミニスト	man who is kind to women	feminist
gādoman	ガードマン	guard or watchman , security guard	guard man*
gāru hanto	ガールハント	"pick up" a girl	girl hunt*
haimisu	ハイミス	single woman aged 25-40	high miss*
naiibu	ナイーブ	pure-minded, fragile person	naive
ōrudo misu	オールドミス	old maid; spinster	old miss*
sarariiman	サラリーマン	male white-collar worker; commuter; office worker	salaryman*
serebu	セレブ	rich people, upper class	celebrity
terebi tarento	テレビタレント	TV personality or celebrity	talent

Home

			English Word
koppu	コップ	glass, not a cup	cup
mikisā	ミキサー	blender	mixer
potto	ポット	thermos bottle or jug	pot
renji	レンジ	oven	kitchen range
sutōbu	ストーブ	heater	stove

Clothing and Fashion

bando	バンド	belt	band
guramā	グラマー	glamor girl; woman with Western figure	glamor
hai sensu	ハイセンス	sense of fashion; wearing the "right" kind of clothing	high sense*
jampā	ジャンパー	windbreaker; half-jacket	jumper
sutairu	スタイル	shape of the body; posture; bearing	style
sumāto	スマート	slim, slender person	smart
waishatsu	ワイシャツ	dress shirt of any color	white shirt

Miscellaneous

apāto	アパート	apartment building (usually a two-story walk up)	apartment
depāto	デパート	department store	department
manshon	マンション	apartment building, more luxurious than an **apāto** (usually a multistory, ferroconcrete building with elevator)	mansion
pinku eiga	ピンク映画	dirty movie	pink movie*
tabako	たばこ	cigarette, pack of cigarettes (not pipe tobacco)	tobacco

* *Reference:* T. E. Huber, "Gaikokujin no Ki ni Suru Nippongo; Imi no Kawatta Gairaigo," **Gengo Seikatsu** 7 (1971): 81-87.

APPENDIX 4

Summary of verb conjugation

Verb Group*	Definition	Dictionary Form		Verb-Infinitive		Polite Present Habitual Future		Polite Past		Polite Negative Present-Habitual Future		-te Form	
Vowel verbs													
-eru**	eat	taberu	食べる	tabe-	食べ	tabemasu	食べます	tabemashita	食べました	tabemasen	食べません	tabete	食べて
-iru	see	miru	見る	mi-	見	mimasu	見ます	mimashita	見ました	mimasen	見ません	mite	見て
Consonant verbs													
-ku	write	kaku	書く	kaki-	書き	kakimasu	書きます	kakimashita	書きました	kakimasen	書きません	kaite	書いて
-gu	hurry	isogu	急ぐ	isogi-	急ぎ	isogimasu	急ぎます	isogimashita	急ぎました	isogimasen	急ぎません	isoide	急いで
-bu	call	yobu	呼ぶ	yobi-	呼び	yobimasu	呼びます	yobimashita	呼びました	yobimasen	呼びません	yonde	呼んで
-mu	drink	nomu	飲む	nomi-	飲み	nomimasu	飲みます	nomimashita	飲みました	nomimasen	飲みません	nonde	飲んで
-ru	return home	kaeru	帰る	kaeri-	帰り	kaerimasu	帰ります	kaerimashita	帰りました	kaerimasen	帰りません	kaette	帰って
vowel + u	buy	kau	買う	kai-	買い	kaimasu	買います	kaimashita	買いました	kaimasen	買いません	katte	買って
-su	speak	hanasu	話す	hanashi-	話し	hanashimasu	話します	hanashimashita	話しました	hanashimasen	話しません	hanashite	話して
-tsu	wait	matsu	待つ	machi-	待ち	machimasu	待ちます	machimashita	待ちました	machimasen	待ちません	matte	待って
Irregular verbs													
	do	suru	する	shi-	し	shimasu	します	shimashita	しました	shimasen	しません	shite	して
	come	kuru	来る	ki-	来	kimasu	来ます	kimashita	来ました	kimasen	来ません	kite	来て

* Includes every type of Japanese verb except that ending in -nu, of which there is just one in the language: shinu, "to die."

** Forms presented in the book but not listed here: tabemasen deshita, tabetai desu, tabemashō.

GLOSSARY

The Glossary (English to Japanese) includes nearly all of the words presented in Chapters 1-9. More than one Japanese word is given where appropriate. Alternative pronunciations are enclosed in brackets. For a subject-guide to vocabulary lists in the text, see page 256.

A

abalone	awabi
about	gurai [kurai]
adult	Otona
aerogram	kōkūshokan
again	mō ichido
airport	kūkō
aloha shirt	araha shatsu
always	itsumo
A.M.	gozen
American	Amerikajin
American consulate	Amerika Ryōjikan
American embassy	Amerika Taishikan
apartment	apāto
apple	ringo
apple pie	appuru pai
April	Shigatsu
art museum	bijutsukan
August	Hachigatsu
Australian	Ōsutorariajin
autumn	aki

B

bacon	bēkon
bad	warui
baggage check room	nimotsu ichiji azukarijo
bamboo craft	takeseihin, takezaiku
banana	banana
bank	ginkō
bank employee	ginkōin
bar	bā
barbershop	rihatsuten, bābā shoppu
bean	ingen
beauty salon	biyōin
beef curry	biifu karē

beefsteak	biifusutēki
beef stew	biifu shichū
beer	biiru
before	mae
begin	hajimeru / hajimemasu
beige	beiju
beverage	nomimono
big	ōkii
bill (check)	o-kanjō
bill (paper money)	satsu
bitter	nigai
black	kuroi
blue	aoi
board (v.)	noru / norimasu
book	hon
book store	hon-ya
boring	tsumaranai, taikutsu (na)
borrow	kariru / karimasu
bowling	bōringu
box	hako
brandy	burandē
bread	pan
brown	chairo(i)
brush painting	sumie
bullet train	shinkansen
bunch	fusa
burdock	gobō
businessman	bijinesuman
bus stop	basu noriba, basu no teiryūjo
busy	isogashii
buy	kau / kaimasu

C

cabbage	kyabetsu
cake	kēki

call	yobu / yobimasu	cucumber	kyūri
camera	kamera	curry rice	karē raisu
Canadian	Kanadajin	customer	o-kyaku
cardigan	kādegan	cutlet	katsuretsu
carrot	ninjin	cutting	katto
cauliflower	karifurawā		
change	o-tsuri	**D**	
change	norikaeru /	dancing	dansu
	norikaemasu	daughter	musume (my);
cherry	sakuranbo		musume-san,
chicken curry	chikin karē		o-jō-san (other's)
child	kodomo (my);	day	hi
	o-ko-san (other's)	day after tomorrow	asatte
Chinese	Chūgokugo	day before yesterday	ototoi
chocolate cake	chokorēto kēki	December	Jūnigatsu
cigarette	tabako	decide	kimeru / kimemasu
close	shimeru /	delicious	oishii
	shimemasu	dentist	haisha
coat	kōto	department store	depāto
cocktail	kakuteru	depressing	uttōshii
cocoa	kokoa	die	shinu / shinimasu
coffee	kōhii	difficult	muzukashii
coffee shop, café	kissaten	dining room	shokudō
coin	-dama	dislike	kirai (na)
coin locker	koin rokkā	do	suru / shimasu
cola	kōra	do (polite)	nasaru / nasaimasu
cold (objects)	tsumetai	door	doa
cold (weather)	samui	dress	doresu
cold wave	kōrudo	dress shirt	waishatsu
combination	mikkusu sandoitchi	drink	nomu / nomimasu
sandwich	[mikkusu sando]	driver	untenshu
come	kuru / kimasu	drug store	kusuriya, yakkyoku
come (polite)	irassharu /		
	irasshaimasu	**E**	
come up	agaru / agarimasu	early	hayai
company president	shachō	easy	yasashii
conductor (train/bus)	shashō	eat	taberu / tabemasu
cooked rice	go-han	eat (polite)	meshiagaru /
cooking	o-ryōri		meshiagarimasu
cool	suzushii	eggplant	nasu
cotton kimono	yukata	eight	hachi
coupon ticket	kaisūken	eight (units)	yattsu
cramped	semai	eighteen	jūhachi
croquette	korokke	eighth day (eight days)	yōka

eight hours	hachi-jikan
eight minutes	hachi-fun [happun]
eight persons	hachi-nin
eighty	hachijū
electric train	densha
eleven	jūichi
eleven hours	jūichi-jikan
English language	Eigo
English person	Igirisujin
English tea	kōcha
enjoyable	tanoshii
enter	hairu / hairimasu
every day	mainichi
every evening	maiban
every month	maitsuki
every morning	maiasa
every night	maiyo
every week	maishū
every year	mainen, maitoshi
exactly	chōdo
exist (animate)	iru / imasu
exist (inanimate)	aru / arimasu
expensive	takai

F

famous	yūmei (na)
fan	sensu
far	tōi
fast	hayai
father	chichi (my); o-tō-san (other's)
February	Nigatsu
fifteen	jūgo
fifth day (five days)	itsuka
fifty	gojū
film	fuirumu
first day	tsuitachi
five	go
five (units)	itsutsu
five hours	go-jikan
five minutes	go-fun
five persons	go-nin
folding screens	byōbu
folk craft	mingeihin

forty	yonjū
four	shi, yo, yon
four (units)	yottsu
four hours	yo-jikan
four minutes	yon-pun
four persons	yo-nin
fourteen	jūshi, jūyon
fourth day (four days)	yokka
free (time)	hima (na)
French language	Furansugo
French person	Fufansujin
Friday	Kinyōbi
fruit	kudamono
fruit stand	kudamonoya

G

German language	Doitsugo
get off	oriru / orimasu
get on	noru / norimasu
gin fizz	jin fuizu
give	ageru / agemasu
give (polite)	sashiageru / sashiagemasu
give (me, please)	kudasai
glad	ureshii
go	iku / ikimasu
golf	gorufu
good	ii
go out	dekakeru / dekakemasu
grape	budō
gray	gurei
green	guriin
green onion	negi, naganegi
green pepper	piiman
grill	guriru

H

hairdye	heyādai
half	hambun
ham	hamu
hamburger	hambāgā
ham sandwich	hamu sandoilchi [ham sando]

handkerchief	**hankachi**
happi coat	**happi**
hard (texture)	**katai**
Hawaiian person	**Hawaijin**
he	**kare**
healthy	**genki (na)**
here	**koko**
home	**uchi, ie**
hospital	**byōin**
hostess	**hosutesu**
hot	**atsui**
hotel	**hoteru**
hotel dining room	**hoteru no shokudō**
how many (units)?	**ikutsu**
how many days?	**nannichi**
how many hours?	**nanjikan**
how many persons?	**nannin**
how much?	**ikura**
hundred	**hyaku**
hundred thousand	**jūman**
hurry	**isogu / isogimasu**
husband	**shujin** (my); **goshujin** (other's)

I

I	**watashi** (less formal); **watakushi** (polite)
ice coffee	**aisu kōhii**
ice cream	**aisukuriimu**
ice cream soda	**aisukuriimu sōda**
inexpensive	**yasui**
information desk	**annaijo**
interesting	**omoshiroi**
Italian language	**Itariago**
Italian person	**Itariajin**

J

jacket	**sebiro, uwagi**
January	**Ichigatsu**
Japan	**Nihon [Nippon]**
Japanese inn	**ryokan**
Japanese language	**Nihongo** **[Nippongo]**
Japanese-style food	**washoku**
Japanese tea	**o-cha**

Japanese wooden doll	**kokeshi**
juice	**jūsu**
July	**Shichigatsu**
June	**Rokugatsu**

K

Kabuki play	**Kabuki**
kimono	**kimono**
kind	**shinsetsu (na)**

L

last evening	**kinō no ban**
last month	**sengetsu**
last night	**kinō no yoru**
last week	**senshū**
last year	**kyonen**
lavender	**rabendā**
learn	**narau / naraimasu**
leave	**deru / demasu**
lend	**kasu / kashimasu**
lettuce	**retasu**
library	**toshokan**
likable	**suki (na)**
listen	**kiku / kikimasu**
(a) little	**sukoshi**
lonely	**sabishii**
long	**nagai**
loquat	**biwa**
low (height)	**hikui**

M

mail (*v*)	**dasu / dashimasu**
make (a telephone call)	**(denwa o) kakeru / kakemasu**
make (cook)	**tsukuru / tsukurimasu**
manicure	**manikyua**
March	**Sangatsu**
marriage	**kekkon**
May	**Gogatsu**
meal	**shokuji**
medical doctor	**isha; o-isha-san** (in addressing)
meet	**au / aimasu**

milk	miruku
million	hyakuman
minutes	-fun [-pun]
Monday	Getsuyōbi
money	o-kane
mother	haha (my);
	o-kā-san (other's)
movie	eiga
movie theater	eigakan
muggy	mushiatsui

N

name	namae
near	chikai
necktie	nekutai
new	atarashii
next month	raigetsu
next week	raishū
next year	rainen
nine	ku, kyū
nine (units)	kokonotsu
nine hours	ku-jikan
nine minutes	kyū-fun
nine persons	kyū-nin
nineteen	jūku, jūkyū
ninety	kyūjū
ninth day (nine days)	kokonoka
no	iie
Noh play	Nō
noodles	soba, udon
November	Jūichigatsu
now	ima
nurse	kangofu;
	kangofu-san
	(in addressing)

O

-o'clock	-ji
October	Jūgatsu
octopus	tako
often	yoku
old (things)	furui
omelet	omuretsu
one	ichi

one (unit)	hitotsu
one-course meal	ippin ryōri
one day	ichinichi
one hour	ichi-jikan
one minute	ippun
one person	hitori
one-way (ticket)	katamichi (kippu)
onion	tamanegi
only	dake
open	akeru / akemasu
orange	orenji
orange (color)	orenji
orange juice	orenji jūsu
over that way	achira
over there	asoko

P

pay	harau / haraimasu
peach	momo
pear	nashi
pearl	shinju
persimmon	kaki
person	hito
phone number	denwa bangō
photo studio	shashin-ya
piano	piano
pie	pai
pile (mountain)	yama
pink	pinku
please	dōzo
(offering something)	
plentiful	ōi
P.M.	gogo
policeman	keikan, o-mawari-san
police substation	kōban, kōbansho
pork cutlet	tonkatsu
postcard	hagaki
post office	yūbinkyoku
potato	jagaimo
pottery	yakimono
practice	renshū
pretty	kirei (na)
public telephone	kōshū denwa
puppet play	Bunraku

Q

quiet	shizuka (na)

R

radio	rajio
radish	daikon
raincoat	reinkōto [renkōto]
razor cut	rezā katto
read	yomu / yomimasu
record	rekōdo
red	akai
require (time)	kakaru / kaimasu
rest	yasumu / yasumi-masu
return (things)	kaesu / kaeshimasu
return home	kaeru / kaerimasu
roast beef	rōsuto biifu
round-trip ticket	ōfuki [kippu]
rum	ramu
Russian language	Roshiago

S

sad	kanashii
sake	o-sake
salad	sarada
salmon roe	ikura
salty	karai
sandals (Japanese style)	zōri
sandwich	sandoitchi [sando]
sash	obi
Saturday	Doyōbi
sausage	sōsēji
say	iu [yū] / iimasu
say (polite)	ossharu / osshaimasu
scarce	sukunai
scarf	sukāfu
school	gakkō
Scotch whiskey	Sukotchi uisukii
sea urchin	uni
seafood curry	shiifūdo karē
second day (two days)	futsuka
secretary	hisho
see	miru / mimasu
send	okuru / okurimasu
September	Kugatsu
set	setto
seven	shichi, nana
seven (units)	nanatsu
seven hours	shichi-jikan
seven minutes	shichi-fun, nana-fun
seven persons	nana-nin, shichi-nin
seventeen	jūshichi, jūnana
seventh day (seven days)	nanoka [nanka]
seventy	nanajū, shichijū
shampoo	shanpū
shave	higesori
she	kanojo
shop owner	shujin
short	mijikai
show	miseru / misemasu
shrimp	ebi
shrine	jinja
sightseeing	kenbutsu
sit	suwaru / suwarimasu
six	roku
six (units)	muttsu
six hours	roku-jikan
six minutes	roppun
six persons	roku-nin
sixteen	jūroku
sixth day (six days)	muika
sixty	rokujū
skating	sukēto
skiing	sukii
skillful	jōzu (na)
skirt	sukāto
slacks	surakkusu
sleep, go to bed	neru / nemasu
slow	osoi
slowly	yukkuri
small	chiisai
soda	sōda
soft	yawarakai
sometimes	tokidoki

son	musuko (my); musuko-san (other's)	television set	terebi
		ten	jū
soup	sūpu	ten (units)	tō
sour	suppai	ten hours	jū-jikan
spacious	hiroi	ten minutes	juppun [jippun]
Spanish language	Supeingo	tennis	tenisu
Spanish person	Supeinjin	ten persons	jū-nin
sports shirt	supōtsu shatsu	tenth day (ten days)	tōka
spring	haru	ten thousand	ichiman
squid	ika	there	soko
stamp	kitte	these days	konogoro
station	eki	thin (the hair)	(kami o) suku / sukimasu
station employee	eki-in		
station store	eki no baiten	think	kangaeru / kangaemasu
stereo	sutereo		
stop	yameru / yamemasu	third day (three days)	mikka
store clerk	ten-in	thirteen	jūsan
straight (liquor)	sutorēto de	thirty	sanjū
strawberry	ichigo	this	kore
student	gakusei	this evening	konban
study	benkyō	this month	kongetsu
style	sutairu	this morning	kesa
subway station	chikatetsu no eki, chikatetsu no noriha	this way	kochira
		this week	konshū
		this year	kotoshi
suit	sūtsu	thousand	sen
summer	natsu	three	san
Sunday	Nichiyōbi	three (units)	mittsu
sweater	sētā	three hours	sanjikan
sweet	amai	three minutes	sanpun
sword	katana	three persons	sannin
		Thursday	Mokuyōbi
		ticket	kippu
T		ticket-selling machine	kenbaiki
talk	hanasu / hanashimasu	ticket window	kippu uriba
		to, as far as	made
tangerine	mikan	today	kyō
tape recorder	tēpu rekōdā	toilet	o-tearai
taxi stand	takushii noriba	tomato	tomato
teach	oshieru / oshiemasu	tomato juice	tomato jūsu
		tomorrow	ashita
teacher	sensei	tomorrow evening	ashita no ban
telephone	kōkanshu, denwa no kōkanshu	tomorrow morning	ashita no asa
operator		tomorrow night	ashita no yoru

tonight	kon-ya	water	o-mizu
toward you	sochira	water and ice	mizuwari de
travel	ryokō	(liquor with)	
trim	suso (dake karu)	watermelon	suika
trousers	zubon	wear	kiru / kimasu
Tuesday	Kayōbi	weather	o-tenki
tuna	maguro	Wednesday	Suiyōbi
tuna (belly flesh)	toro	Western-style food	yōshoku
turn	magaru / magarimasu	what?	nan(i)
		what day?	nannichi
twelve	jūni	what day of the week?	nan-yōbi
twelve hours	jūni-jikan	what kind of?	donna
twentieth day	hatsuka	what month?	nangatsu
(twenty days)		what number?	nanban
twenty	nijū	what time?	nanji
twenty-thousand	niman	wheat noodles	soba
two	ni	when?	itsu
two (units)	futatsu	where?	doko
two hours	ni-jikan	which?	dore
two minutes	ni-fun	which way?	dochira
two persons	futari	whiskey	uisukii
two thousand	nisen	whiskey soda	uisukii sodā
		white	shiroi
U		white-collar employee	sarariiman
unappetizing	mazui	wife	kanai (my);
underpants	pantsu		oku-san (other's)
undershirt	shatsu	window	mado
understand	wakaru / wakarimasu	winter	fuyu
university	daigaku	wonderful	suteki (na)
unskilled	heta (na)	woodblock print	hanga
useless	dame (na)	write	kaku / kakimasu
usually	taitei		
		Y	
V		year before last	ototoshi
vegetable	yasai	yellow	kiiroi
vegetable stand	yaoya	yen	-en
vodka	uokka	yes	hai, ē
		yesterday	kinō
W		yesterday morning	kinō no asa
wait	matsu / machimasu	you	anata
walk	aruku / arukimasu	young	wakai
(a) walk	sanpo		
warm	atatakai [attakai]	**Z**	
wash	arau / araimasu	zero	rei, maru, zero

INDEX

VOCABULARY LISTS